Speeding Financial Inclusion

Published by Academic Foundation
in association with

SKOCH
DEVELOPMENT FOUNDATION

Skoch Development Foundation
www.skoch.org

Sameer Kochhar is President of Skoch Development Foundation—a not-for-profit Section 25 company—and has been passionately working towards promoting participatory democracy, empowerment and bringing improvements in delivery systems. He is CEO, Skoch Consultancy Services and is an industry veteran with a multifaceted career spanning over two and a half decades. He has been India strategy and management consultant to several Fortune 500 as well as large Indian companies for over a decade. He is also Chief Editor of Inclusion—a quarterly publication focused on development economics issues. He is considered to be one of the most respected independent voices on inclusive development and citizenship issues in India. He is a member of several expert groups and committees and his research opinions and writings have shaped many a public policy dialogue. He is also a Member of the Expert Group constituted by the Ministry of Panchayati Raj, Government of India advocating a case for strengthening of Panchayati Raj Institutions (village councils), and urban local bodies. He has written extensively on areas of emerging management practices, mergers and acquisitions, Indian IT industry, e-Governance, Panchayati Raj, and, ICT for development. He has recently published with Academic Foundation, New Delhi three widely acclaimed books titled: Infrastructure and Governance (2008); Financial Inclusion (2009); and, Urban Renewal: Policy and Response (2009).

Speeding Financial Inclusion

Sameer Kochhar

ACADEMIC FOUNDATION
NEW DELHI

First published in 2009
by

ACADEMIC FOUNDATION
4772-73 / 23 Bharat Ram Road, (23 Ansari Road),
Darya Ganj, New Delhi - 110 002 (India).
Phones : 23245001 / 02 / 03 / 04.
Fax : +91-11-23245005.
E-mail : books@academicfoundation.com
www. academicfoundation.com

in association with
Skoch Development Foundation
www.skoch.org
E-mail : info@skoch.org

Cataloging in Publication Data--DK
Courtesy: D.K. Agencies (P) Ltd. <docinfo@dkagencies.com>

Kochhar, Sameer.
Speeding financial inclusion /Sameer Kochhar.
p. cm.
In Indian context.
ISBN 13: 9788171887910
ISBN 10: 8171887910

1. Finance--Social aspects--India. 2. Financial services industry--India. 3. Rural poor--India. 4. Rural credit--India. 5. India--Economic policy--1991- I. Title.

DDC 332.0954 22

Typeset and cover design: Italics India, New Delhi.
Printed and bound in India.

Contents

Acknowlegements

We would like to thank all the people who gave us constructive inputs through the study conducted over the last six months. It was logically a daunting task that involved travelling to various cities, towns and villages, holding one-on-one discussions, national consultation, research meetings and interacting with various stakeholders.

We are grateful to Dr. C. Rangarajan, Chairman, Economic Advisory Council to the Prime Minister for mentoring and being an inspiration for the study and chairing the national consultation on the draft report at Mumbai. The study could not be complete without Dr. K.C. Chakrabarty who very kindly agreed to write an Introduction to the study and also participated in the national consultation at Mumbai. We truly appreciate Mr. R. Chandrashekhar, Secretary, Department of Information Technology for chairing the 2nd research meeting and presenting a paper on "Universal Financial Access".

We would like to thank Prof. Deepak B. Phatak, IIT-B, Mumbai for actively participating and conducting the national consultation sessions in Mumbai and also hosting our first research meeting on IIT-B campus. More importantly, we also thank him for keeping on inspiring us to think of the poor. We also thank Mr. H. Krishnamurthy, Indian Institute of Science for getting the distillate out of the discussions during the national consultation at Mumbai.

Special thanks are due to all the people who participated in research meetings.

Notably, Prof. Ashok Jhunjhunwala, IIT-Madras; Mr. Anandi Lal, Dena Bank; Ms. Lalitha Venkatesan, NABARD; Ms. Saroj Dikle, Life Insurance Corporation; Mr. V. Ramkumar, State Bank of India; Mr. Anurag Gupta, ZERO Mass Foundation; Mr. Matteo Ciampo, Eko India Financial Services; Mr. Mahesh Jain, Integra Microsystems; Mr. S.P. Singh, Punjab

National Bank; Mr. S. Thyagarajan, College of Agricultural Banking (RBI); Mr. M. Moni, National Informatics Centre; Mr. C.S. Ghosh, Bandhan Microfinance; Mr. Navin Anand, UNDP, Mr. Anand Kumar, UNDP; Ms. Monika Khanna, UNDP. We also thank UNDP Solution Exchange Community for making the e-Discussion possible.

Abbreviations

BC	Business Correspondent
BCSBI	Banking Codes and Standards Board of Indian
BF	Business Facilitator
BPL	Below Poverty Line
CIBIL	Credit Information Bureau (India) Limited
CMIE	Centre for Monitoring Indian Economy
EBT	Electronic Benefit Transfer
FIPF	Financial Inclusion Promotion & Development Fund
FITF	Financial Inclusion Technology Fund
FIU	Financial Intelligence Unit
FRBM	Fiscal Responsibility and Budget Management
GDP	Gross Domestic Product
GoI	Government of India
IBA	Indian Banks' Association
ICT	Information and Communication Technologies
IDRBT	Institute for Development and Research in Banking Technology
ICRIER	Indian Council for Research on International Economic Relations
IGIDR	Indira Gandhi Institute of Development Research
IISc	Indian Institute of Science
IIT	Indian Institute of Technology
IRDA	Insurance Regulatory and Development Authority
JLG	Joint Liability Groups
KYC	Know Your Customer

MDG	Millennium Development Goal
MFI	Micro Finance Institution
MoCIT	Ministry of Communications and IT
MoF	Ministry of Finance
MoPR	Ministry of Panchayati Raj
MoRD	Ministry of Rural Development
MPFI	Mobile Payment Forum of India
NABARD	National Bank for Agriculture and Rural Development
NaMFI	National Mission on Financial Inclusion
NBFC	Non-Banking Financial Companies
NCAER	National Council of Applied Economic Research
NER	North Eastern Region
NGO	Non-Governmental Organisation
NIPFP	National Institute of Public Finance and Policy
NPA	Non-Performing Asset
NREGA	National Rural Employment Guarantee Act
NREGS	National Rural Employment Guarantee Scheme
NRFIP	National Rural Financial Inclusion Plan
PMGSY	Pradhan Mantri Gram Sadak Yojana
PNB	Punjab National Bank
RBI	Reserve Bank of India
RRB	Regional Rural Bank
RSBY	Rashtriya Swasthya Bima Yojana
SBI	State Bank of India
SDF	Skoch Development Foundation
SEBI	Securities and Exchange Board of India
SHG	Self Help Groups
TRAI	Telecom Regulatory Authority of India
UNDP	United Nations Development Programme

Preface

The Indian economy has done well in recent years. The average rate of growth of the economy in the last five years has been 8.5 per cent. During the three year period 2005-06 to 2007-08, the annual growth rate exceeded 9 per cent. However, the growth rate slowed down to 6.7 per cent in 2008-2009, primarily due to external factors. The growth rate in the current year (2009-10) is likely to remain more or less at the same level. Even as we address the immediate problems, we must keep in mind the medium and long-term goals and the constraints that need to be overcome in order to achieve these goals. Inclusive growth, as you all know, has become almost an expression of common usage now. Inclusive growth attempts to bridge the various divides in an economy and society, between the rich and the poor, rural and urban populace and between one region and another. This is a formidable task. The process of growth has to be such that all sections of society benefit from the growth process and that is the essence of inclusive growth.

In the post-independent economic history of our country, 1991 is an important landmark. This was the year in which the country faced an acute economic crisis, triggered largely by a severe problem of balance of payments. The response to the crisis was to put in place a set of policies aimed at stabilisation and introducing structural reforms. These structural reforms, introduced since 1992-93, have been intended to remove the rigidities that had entered into our economic system. The primary objective of the new economic policy was to improve productivity and efficiency of the system by injecting a greater element of competition. This break with the past happened in three important ways. First, the unnecessary controls and licences were dismantled and entrepreneurs were given greater freedom to decide what to produce, how to produce and where to produce. The second challenge was to reverse the extreme bias towards state ownership of enterprises. Some of the areas exclusively reserved for the public sector have now been thrown open to the private sector. But there are still large areas in which the public sector still plays an important part and it will have to compete in those areas with the private sector. As has been somewhat paradoxically said, "more market does not mean less Government but only different Government." Nevertheless, I think the role and the importance attached to public enterprises has undergone a change and that was the second break with the past. The third was the greater integration of the Indian economy with the rest of the world. Such integration has its pros and cons, but I think by integrating with the rest of the world, India is proving that through productivity and efficiency improvements, it can stand competition with the rest of the world.

That the content and approach of our economic reforms is in the right direction is evident from the rapid progress that we have made in recent years. In the decade before the introduction of the reforms, the average rate of growth of the economy was 5.6 per cent. But in the period since 1992-1993, the average rate of growth has been 6.8 per cent and more recently, we have been able to show a significant uptrend in the growth rate.

However, there are many imperatives in the way forward. We need to sustain the present rate of growth, if not accelerate it to higher levels. We need to translate growth into poverty reducing growth, a process of growth to which the poor can contribute and from which the poor can also benefit. We need to expand the employment opportunities and improve productivity across all sectors of the economy. We need to narrow economic disparities across and within states without compromising on efficiency. We need to improve the social indicators. India still ranks a low 128th in the United Nation Development Programme's Human Development Index, coming in the bottom one-third of the league of nations. Thus, the agenda for achieving growth and poverty reduction is formidable.

One aspect of inclusive growth is financial inclusion. The process of financial inclusion is an attempt to bring within the ambit of the organised financial system the weaker and vulnerable sections of society. Financial inclusion can be defined as the delivery of credit and other financial services at an affordable cost to the vast sections of the disadvantaged and low income groups. The various financial services include savings, credit, insurance and payments and remittance facilities. It will be wrong to classify all those who are not borrowing from the organised financial system as excluded. What is relevant is that whether those who need credit and who want credit from the organised system are included in the ambit of the financial system or not. The criterion for being bankable should not be interpreted narrowly to exclude the vast majority. The objective of financial inclusion is to extend the scope of activities of the organised financial system to include, within its ambit, people with low incomes. Through graduated credit, attempts must be made to lift the poor so that they come out of poverty. Financial inclusion may, therefore, be defined as the process of enabling access to timely and adequate credit and other financial services by vulnerable groups, such as weaker sections and low income groups at affordable cost.

We all are familiar with the extent of exclusion. The National Sample Survey data reveals that 45.9 million farmer households in the country, i.e., 51.4 per cent of the nearly 89.3 million total households do not access credit either from institutional or non-institutional sources. Nearly 51 per cent do not have access to any credit, formal or informal. More importantly, despite the vast network of rural branches, only 27 per cent of the total farm households are indebted to formal sources; of them, one-third also borrow from informal sources. Besides, there are vast regional differences. There are parts of the country where more than 95 per cent of the farm households do not get any credit from institutional or non-institutional sources. Thus, apart from the fact that exclusion itself is large, it also varies widely across regions, social groups and asset holdings. The poorer the group, the greater is the exclusion.

The question that is before us is how to extend the scope of activities of the organised financial system to include low income groups. Institutions which currently provide credit in the rural areas include the rural and semi-urban branches of commercial banks, regional rural banks, cooperative societies and micro-finance institutions. What is required is not to create any new institution for providing credit to the excluded, but to enable the existing institutions to extend their outreach. There is a need to find ways and means to effect improvements within the existing financial credit delivery mechanism and evolve new models for extending their outreach. In a broad sense, we need to address issues on the supply as well as the demand side. The formal banking system, the rural cooperatives, and non-governmental organisations (NGOs) must be strengthened organisationally to extend their outreach. The financially excluded sections require products which are customised to meet their needs.

Financial exclusion is also caused by demand side factors. Unless steps are taken on the demand side, i.e., in the real sectors, mere supply side solutions will not solve the problem. Credit is necessary for this but not sufficient. Credit has to be integrated and made a part of an overall programme aimed at improving the productivity and income of small farmers and other poor households. Putting in place an appropriate credit delivery system to meet the needs of all marginal and small farmers must go hand in hand with the efforts to improve the productivity of such farm households. So, it is extremely important that we integrate the credit delivery system of the organised financial system with the programmes and policies being implemented by the government to improve the lot of the poor. There are number of programmes initiated by the Government and if there is a significant degree of coordination between the organised financial system and these programmes, I think we will have the best results, both from the point of view of improved delivery of credit as well as the effectiveness of such programmes.

There are many things that can be said in order to improve the organisational efficiency of banks and other financial institutions. Importantly, there is a need for a change in the attitude of the people who serve in the banks. Empathy with the poor, especially with those who need credit, must be established and here, perhaps, improved training will help. Also, rural branches must go beyond providing credit and extend a helping hand to farmers in terms of advice on a wide variety of matters relating to agriculture and other allied activities. We should look up on the rural branches of commercial banks as not merely pure financial institutions but also as advisory institutions. There is no denying that we need to open more branches in the rural areas as there are still pockets which are unbanked in our country. And, in these areas, the traditional brick and mortar branches may still be needed. There is also the need for simplification of procedures in order to enable farmers to obtain credit more easily from the organised system.

In establishing a strong relationship between the organised financial system, like commercial banks, and those people who need credit, the Bank-SHG linkage scheme is of extreme importance. Self-help groups have become a very established institution in our country. Here, I am indeed happy that I have had some role to play in the initial evolution of the relationship between banks and self-help groups (SHGs). It was in 1992 when I asked the banks to provide credit to such SHGs even though they were not legally recognised. The SHGs are still not recognised as legal entities. To go back, I think the experience with the working of the self-help groups has been extremely good. Their repayment ethics has been good and they have been able to repay promptly loans granted by commercial banks. There are of course a lot of improvements that are required. We need to increase in the number of SHGs in all parts of the country. Today, they are largely concentrated in the Southern region. Also, the SHGs need to graduate from one level to another level. So far, they have been largely devoted to meeting the consumer credit needs of their members. It is only now that some of them are progressing towards becoming productive organisations. I think that this is a development which is extremely important. While recognising that SHG members do need consumer credit, we cannot keep them at that level. It is important that such SHGs become productive entities also, contributing to the local economy.

Then there is the question about the rate of interest. Some state governments have provided subsidy in terms of reducing the rate of interest offered to SHGs. I feel that the rate at which commercial banks even normally lend to a SHG is reasonable and the interest rate subsidy is not really required. In fact, if state governments do want to support SHGs, they should do so in trying to help the SHGs organise themselves better, provide marketing facilities and provide other kinds of advice on productive activities. I think the role of the state government will be better served in providing these necessary additional facilities, which will make SHGs more efficient rather than providing interest rate subsidy.

There is also the question of federating the SHGs. To some extent, there has been progress in this area in some states where the SHGs have been federated at the village level, at the *taluk* level and also at the district level. Here, I feel it is important that the SHGs should see a felt need for federating, it should not be imposed from outside. If SHGs find it worthwhile to come together so that they can reap some synergic benefits, then this should be promoted. Here, the role of such federations must be more in the form of a facilitator rather than as a credit intermediary. SHGs should obtain credit directly from commercial banks and federations must facilitate this process rather than becoming another intermediary in the chain itself.

The other important thing is the role of the business correspondent and business facilitator. The business facilitator and the correspondent model needs to be effectively implemented. In order to increase the outreach of the banking sector, the Reserve Bank of India permitted banks to use the services of specified institutions as intermediaries for providing banking services. However, this scheme has not taken off. This model has a high potential. Banks must take the initiative to remove the obstacles that come in their way for a more extended use of facilitators and correspondents. The list of people who can become facilitators can be expanded to include even people like ex-servicemen. There is also the possibility of allowing Section 25 companies to become correspondents. There is also the possibility of allowing different types of institutions, like village cooperative credit societies, to become facilitators or correspondents for commercial banks. Therefore, we have to explore the possibility of finding appropriate institutions that can serve as a good link between commercial banks' rural branches and farm households.

There have been several studies which have been done in order to strengthen the village credit cooperative societies. Many of them are in a moribund state. We need to revive them. The Vaidyanathan Committee had made specific recommendations for reviving both short-term and long-term cooperative credit and these also should be addressed so that the cooperative credit movement again becomes a vibrant movement.

But the critical question, and one that the study by Sameer Kochhar has also raised, is the cost of such intermediation through business correspondents and who is to bear this cost. As the study reveals, there is a cost involved in such intermediation and if this cost is not covered, then the viability of the system of business correspondents itself is in question. Let us recognise the fact that by introducing the business correspondent model, we are ensuring a closer relationship between the poor people and the organised financial system.

Today, in the task of making banking services available to everyone, technology has come to have an important role to play. It is technology that has made it possible for business correspondents to deal with commercial banks. The required outreach into the interiors with low operational cost is only possible with the use of appropriate technology. But this technology, though simple in one way, still has a cost and therefore, the question that arises is who will meet the cost. As the report of Kochhar shows that while alternative technologies—smart card, plastic card and so on—are available, there is a significant viability gap and unless this viability gap is filled in by the banks or by any other mechanism, schemes to widen financial outreach will not take off. The Report on Financial Inclusion had suggested two separate funds—one for the promotion of financial inclusion and the other as a technology fund. While the former must be utilised for the promotion of the business facilitator and correspondent model as well as for the promotion of SHGs, the latter can be used primarily to help the banks meet the cost for inducting the technology necessary for these models to succeed.

In a sense, what we really need today is the development of a variety of institutions. As far as commercial banks are concerned, the two pillars which will help the organised banking system to widen its outreach is the strengthening of the Bank-SHG linkage scheme and the strengthening of the business correspondent model. But the larger issue that remains is that we really need to see economic growth and social development going hand in hand. Social development cannot be sustained for a long period unless there is strong economic growth. But if economic growth by itself does not result in social development, it may not be of much use. Therefore, the two must go hand in hand. Economic growth and social development are the two legs on which a nation must walk. Any strategy of development which ignores any one leg will mean that the country will only limp along. Equity and efficiency should not be posed as opposing considerations. They must be woven together to produce a coherent pattern of growth. Here, financial inclusion has an important role to play. Financial inclusion is no longer an option but a compulsion.

C. Rangarajan
Chairman, Economic Advisory Council to the
Prime Minister, Government of India

Introduction

Financial inclusion is not only the process of ensuring access to financial services or making available timely and adequate credit when needed by vulnerable groups, such as weaker sections and low income groups, at an affordable cost. In our context, definition of financial inclusion is much wider. It is not only providing accessibility of the entire range of financial products and services, it must also be appropriate, fair and transparent. In that sense, we can say that 95 per cent of the population is financially excluded, with most of us not knowing what an appropriate financial product is suitable for us. So, we have to go a long way forward. Today, what we are seeking to do is first improving access to various financial products and services for the entire population and ensuring that such access is provided by mainstream institutional players. Enabling people to get credit from small institutions, moneylenders and the like is not financial inclusion. Access has to be through mainstream institutional players and only then such access will be fair, transparent and cost-effective.

Then we have a question: what does financial inclusion means? The first thing is a check-in account, what we in the system call a no-frills account. And the next stage is immediate credit. Today, what the poor wants is accessibility to immediate credit. As most of the data shows that 80 per cent of the credit requirement of the poor is not for business or entrepreneurship but, it is for meeting a financial emergency, like health, or urgent domestic needs. While the Reserve Bank of India in 2005 facilitated that every no-frills account can be opened with a readymade overdraft, the question that arises is how many banks have opened a no-frills account with a readymade overdraft facility. This immediate credit stage is followed by introduction of various savings products, i.e., other types of savings, followed by remittances and payments services. This is followed by insurance, especially health insurance, mortgage, life insurance, housing loans and then by financial advisory services.

Entrepreneurship credit comes at the last. Today, if we are saying that people have to be made creditworthy and 'financially included' and that is how productivity will improve, we have to go through all these stages and we have a long way to cover.

This brings us to the next question: who are the financially excluded? Again, they are basically the underprivileged sections of the society, i.e., farmers, small vendors, agricultural or industrial labourers, people engaged in unorganised sectors, unemployed people, women, children, old people and the physically challenged. The extent of financial exclusion become clear from these figures: only 40 per cent of the people have a check-in account, 20 per cent have taken life insurance products, 0.6 per cent have taken non-life insurance products; only 2 per cent have access to credit cards. This gives us the scope of business opportunities that are there if we can reach out to all the people. Today, geographically, only 5.2 per cent of the country's villages have a bank branch.

It is not that efforts have not been made earlier to promote financial inclusion. One of the prime aims of the cooperative movement was bringing financial inclusion. The setting up of State Bank of India in 1956, the nationalisation of banks, the introduction of the Lead Bank Scheme, establishing regional rural banks, evaluation of the service area approach and formation of self-help groups were all steps taken to take banking services to the general masses. But despite such measures, only 10 per cent of the population has access to the institutional credit system. A major reason for our failure to promote financial inclusion has been technology. Without technology we cannot reach out to the people. Banking technology is only of recent origin and business delivery model is yet to evolve.

Today, it is clear that we will not be able to promote financial inclusion with a branch-based delivery mechanism. We have to experiment with new types of delivery mechanisms, what we can call the ICT-based delivery mechanism. Here, the problem is that we do not have a business model as to how such a mechanism will be viable. One must remember here that giving a subsidy does not necessarily lead to a better delivery mechanism. So, it is important that any service that seeks to cover the poor and the excluded must be at an affordable cost but never at a loss. We must not exploit the poor, but he must pay the full cost, otherwise there will be leakages. Any such delivery mechanism will be ineffective and the system will be doing greatest disservice to the poor. When we say that we must give the credit to poor at a cheaper rate, we have to realise that if the formal system fails to give credit to the excluded, the alternative is a far costlier option.

Today, our focus is on financial inclusion and inclusive growth. The 11th Five Year Plan also talks about inclusive growth. Inclusive growth cannot come without financial inclusion. Today, globally, the mainstream financial institutions have realised that the poor are bankable. And the technology to make this possible is also there. Here, I feel that the banking correspondent model is one of the most revolutionary reforms which have taken place in our banking system. However, it is one that we are not taking the full advantage of. Under the KYC/GCC guidelines, the poor need not go every time for a transaction to a bank branch. For opening branches in unbanked rural centres, the rules have also been liberalised. Similarly, we have a liberalised policy for ATMs. Today, no licence is needed for setting up ATMs. But the ATMs will work only if bank have customers. Thus, we have introduced technology into our products and services, allowed prepaid cards and mobile banking, allowed regional rural banks and cooperative banks to sell insurance and financial products, and set up two special funds to promote inclusion, but the results are not there. We have opened lots of no-frills accounts, but not even 1 per cent of such accounts have been extended overdrafts despite the rules allowing this. Simply opening a no-frills account is not financial inclusion. It is just the beginning.

The available statistics and this study reveal that we have opened over 28.23 million no-frills accounts, but less than 11 per cent of them are active. Opening no-frills accounts will not give any help to the poor if they do not conduct any transactions. Today, the number of rural bank branches is only 31,727 as against more than 600,000 villages in the country. Similarly, the number of ATMs is 44,857 with a majority of them being in metros and urban centres. Again, there are 470,237 points of sale (PoS) but these are of little use to the rural poor as they cannot deliver cash, which is what they need. Today, a bank branch covers a population of 16,000. So, it is clear that bank branch-based delivery model will not work. We have to go for a different delivery mechanism.

So what are the problems and difficulties? The problem is that while there are islands of excellence, large ocean of deprivation and non-performance remain. It is clear that scaling-up of activities is just not possible. This is because of the fact that transaction costs are high. But, here it should be clear that such costs should be shared by all stakeholders. It must be shared by the state if it feels that it will lead to development. It has to be shared by the bank, provided they feel that there is a future business in this. It must be borne by the customer also if he gets the banking service or product he needs at his doorstep. The key here is to effectively work out this cost. Today, with the technology we have on our side, we can provide all state services and benefits directly to the poor. But there is no reason why the banks should not be paid for this as it helps the state to reduce its cost of administration of such service. Similarly, if a bank feels that this will become a profitable business in future, it should be first prepared to invest in this business. So, it is important that we work out an appropriate business model for promoting financial inclusion.

It is true that the existing banking correspondent model is too restrictive. So changes are to be made in the existing guidelines to make it more flexible and operative. But easing the policy is only one part of it. For inclusion to succeed, we need to be clear that we want inclusion to happen and we are ready to work for it. We may give everything but if we don't have the determination and involvement and if we do not believe that it is a viable business, we will not succeed. Strong collaboration among banks, technical service providers, BC service providers is what is required. Currently, this is lacking. Further, if we believe inclusive growth and financial inclusion is part of the development process, without the involvement of the state at the implementation (local) level, it will not succeed. Thus, in Punjab National Bank, when we started doing financial inclusion, we started with 30 pilot projects and in one year we could open only 2 lakh no-frills accounts. But in Rajasthan when we co-opted the state government, we opened 26 lakh no-frills accounts in just 40 days. Also, given the size and scale of the task on hand, it is important that big players in the technological field become part of the process. Their interest in this area is vital. We require much larger institutional players in the area of technology, research and development, and for evolving cost-effective business solutions to ensure success of financial inclusion.

Today, when we are in the midst of a global meltdown it is the right time to focus on financial inclusion. The meltdown globally has brought more focus on inclusive growth. Today, everybody's attention has shifted from the West to the East, from the US/Europe to India, China and Asia, and this is an opportunity. Focus on domestic consumption and investment—this will not come without linking the people with the banking system. Focus on increased social sector spending—if we want to make spending more productive and more efficient, its delivery has to be through a bank account. Today, everybody is saying that we must give subsidies directly to the poor. In fact, Dr. Meghnad Desai, the noted economist said that everything should be given to the poor in cash and put directly into their bank accounts. This is because this is much more beneficial to the poor. So, let us all come together and give financial inclusion a big push.

I must commend Sameer Kochhar on his out-of-the-box approach which has delivered some critical insights in the form of this study. Reflective of his commitment towards the cause of financial inclusion, the recommendations are focused on speeding the process and are worthy of consideration.

It is time to let the inclusion engine start, allow it to gather speed and accelerate the process. Financial inclusion is necessary not only for the poor, it is a must for ensuring the sustainability of our society.

K.C. Chakrabarty

Deputy Governor, Reserve Bank of India

1 Why This Study

The idea of this study began to germinate earlier this year when Skoch Development Foundation (SDF), a not-for-profit Section 25 company, went to seek tax exemption. The concerned official in the division desired an explanation as to why exemption was being sought. It was submitted that SDF aims to work for digital, social and financial inclusion. The officer replied that such exemptions were granted only to those who work for the poor—how does merely providing bank accounts eradicate poverty? This was surprising enough and it took a while to explain how the other two objectives of digital and social inclusion were interlinked and how this was linked to livelihood and poverty alleviation. The result: submission was accepted. This entire episode, in fact, left us wondering whether these linkages were as obvious to others as they were to us?

The second and more recent catalyst, well after financial inclusion had been declared a goal, was a meeting with a senior government functionary. He mentioned the feedback on financial inclusion from two senior persons, one from a large consulting firm and the other a well-respected economist. These two gentlemen were of the opinion that financial inclusion was slow in happening because of the Know Your Customer (KYC) norms. This was quite a shocker. In contrast, during several traverses in recent years, Skoch has found that KYC guidelines in rural India were so simple that practically anybody could open a bank account and while there were many reasons for the current model not working at the desired pace, KYC norms in rural India were the least of them. The head of a large public sector undertaking, who was also present in that meeting, concurred with this view. The government functionary too agreed that at times, policy makers get only academic inputs that may not be entirely correct and there was a felt need for inputs based on field experience and ground realities.

Somewhere, it was felt that Skoch's anthropological, touchy-feely approach may actually be one good instrumentality in presenting the ground situation.

The past several years have seen the words 'financial inclusion' and 'inclusive growth' becoming part of the common man's glossary as well as a factor in the development agenda, cutting across the whole spectrum. In the same period, quite a bit of experimentation has happened across the country and multiple stakeholders have tried to contribute in their own ways.

The learning from various experiments undertaken in past few years provides us knowledge about the factors of success as well as failures. At this juncture, it is important to take a consolidated view of all the learnings so as to fill in the gaps and suggest a common path to speed up financial inclusion.

Every Skoch summit has deliberated on social, digital and financial inclusion. Skoch has also been credited with having organised the only conference in the North Eastern Region (NER) on financial and digital inclusion in 2006. This was possibly the first conference in NER, where the government system and banking system came together. There, it emerged that at the grassroots, the lines are really blurring and social spending schemes need to be better targeted through the banking system. So, if there is a NREGA payment then it is better served if it goes through the banking and the post office system, so that there are fewer leakages. It was a long journey from 2006 till about late 2008 when that recommendation was actually accepted, and it was advised that NREGA payments should be done only through banks and the post office system in conjunction. A few months ago, Skoch Development Foundation got a reference from the Prime Minister's Economic Advisory Council asking for feedback on how to further strengthen various Bharat Nirman schemes. Skoch thanked them for having acknowledged, accepted and implemented the earlier recommendation on NREGA payments, being routed through the banking and the post office system. However, these payments are getting delayed for two reasons. One is that either the banks are unwilling to cope with the load or they are unable to cope with the load. Just look at the plight of a bank, which has a small moffusil, rural kind of a branch where they would, may be, get 70 or 80 customers in a day, and suddenly a NREGA muster roll has to be paid, with upwards of 500 beneficiaries seeking their payments turning up on the same day week after week. How do you cater to such a situation? Can the BC model help here?

Key Stakeholders

Government

- Planning Commission
- MoCIT
- MoRD
- MoPR
- MoF
- Economic Advisory Council
- FIU

Regulators

- RBI
- IRDA
- TRAI
- SEBI

Civil Society

- NGOs
- MPFI
- e-Communities

Academia

- IIT
- IISc

Players

- Banks
- NBFCs
- Insurance Companies
- Market Players
- Pension Funds
- Postal System

Institutions & Think Tanks

- NABARD
- Banking Codes and Standards Board of India
- IDRBT
- NIPFP
- IGIDR
- ICRIER, NCAER, CMIE, etc.
- BCG etc.

Industry

- Technology Providers, (FINO, A Little World, Atom, Nokia, Intel, etc.)
- BCs & BFs
- ICT industry
- Telcos

The other problem, of course, is that NREGA as a scheme does not provide for any money to handle the transaction fee. Why would the banks want to undertake this responsibility given the costs? All banks are commercial entities; they have shareholders to answer to; the bank chairman's career graph depends on what the bank's bottomline looks like. They have to make some money in the process of handling NREGA payments, which entail very, very small amounts that just come in and go out of the bank. Somebody working under NREGA is unlikely to have a substantial savings account. Only in states like Andhra Pradesh, has the state government been proactive and provided for 2 per cent of the money to be given to the banks for handling NREGA payments. In other states, this is not the case. So, viability is a big issue and a recurrent one in the various discussions and meetings we had.

There is not a single study in the country which brings together all the aspects of financial inclusion, whether it is regulatory, technology or business, and there have been so many pilots, so many banks, so many insurance companies. There are some wonderful stories, some relating to SHGs and MFIs, some to banks themselves. The learning is very rich so nothing really needs to be invented. All the invention has already happened, what we really need to do is to see why it is not happening faster and better. Can we read all these clauses together and can we make these things move? Our study began to take shape.

The study examines the possible ways to accelerate financial inclusion. To do any such study, one has to first define who the stakeholders are: *viz.*, banks, NBFCs, insurance companies, market players, pension funds, postal system, then you have the regulators such as Reserve Bank of India (RBI), Insurance Regulatory and Development Authority (IRDA), Telecom Regulatory Authority of India (TRAI), and Securities and Exchange Board of India (SEBI); institutions and think tanks, and certainly the government. So we believe unless all these stakeholders come together and there is some kind of a broad consensus on what needs to be done, the purpose of the study would not be adequately served. Poverty alleviation is no more a slogan. It is something which has got no colour either politically; there is no dispute that anybody has on it, just the paths taken to that may be different. The differences can be addressed through a consultative participative kind of a process. This is just a humble attempt in that direction.

In order to suggest a common strategy, Skoch undertook a nationwide multi-stakeholder study entitled "National Study on Speeding Financial Inclusion". The study entailed one-on-one interviews; field visits as well as research meetings of practitioners and domain experts; e-discussions, apart from published literature scan, including the study of RBI, government circulars and so on. The e-discussion was held on Solution Exchange[1] and provided key insights to enrich our analysis.

Finally, the draft report was circulated amongst domain experts and also presented to nearly 300 experts from across India who had assembled for the 20th Skoch Summit on July 16-17, 2009 in Mumbai.

1. *www.solutionexchange-un.net.in*

This volume is the result of those many deliberations at various levels and in various parts of the country. Chapter 2 looks at the linkages between financial inclusion and poverty alleviation. The policy measures taken by the government towards financial inclusion are discussed in Chapter 3. Chapter 4 examines the cost of providing financial access in the shape of no-frills accounts. Clearly, as we have repeatedly said, financial inclusion is much more than just the opening of bank accounts. Chapter 5 looks at the need to create awareness and widen product offerings to serve the needs of the poor, both rural and urban, within the framework of inclusive economics. A summary of stakeholder discussions is presented in Chapter 6 as per the research questions. Chapter 7 puts together the recommendations that emerge from the analysis and discussion. This is followed by a section of case studies and best practices.

2 Financial Inclusion and Poverty Alleviation

Financial inclusion unfortunately has become synonymous with the opening of bank accounts. It needs to be much more. We found a clear differentiation between bank accounts linked with livelihood and those just opened for the sake of opening a bank account. An analysis of 50 lakh individual, no-frill accounts revealed that the average balance in livelihood-linked accounts was about Rs. 11,000 while in the others, the average balance was just Rs. 176. It does appear that the BC channel has been reduced to Electronic Benefit Transfer (EBT)[1] channel so that the goal of developmental banking, *viz.*, poverty alleviation, is not being achieved.

In the course of our discussions and research, it soon became clear that, even to the most erudite of people, the linkage between financial inclusion and poverty alleviation was far from clear. History shows that economic growth is the most effective way to reduce poverty. However, economic growth can still leave many people in persistent poverty if they do not have the necessary capacity to participate in and benefit from the growth process. Although the chosen and conventional approaches to tackling poverty and other Millennium Development Goals (MDGs) are useful and necessary, they are not sufficient to address the challenge. Financial inclusion offers incremental and complementary solutions to tackle poverty, to promote inclusive development and to address the MDGs. Some even refer to financial inclusion as a 'quasi-public good', saying that there is substantial evidence that a well-functioning financial system fosters faster and more equitable growth. Access to financial services allows the poor to save money outside the house safely. This brings prosperity over a period of time.[2]

---

1. NREGA payments are an example of EBT.
2. Kelkar, Vijay (2008). "Financial Inclusion for Inclusive Growth," *N.P. Sen Memorial Lecture* at Administrative Staff College of India, Hyderabad, January 13, p.8.

Many studies on poverty indicate that, one of the reasons poor households are unable to participate in the development process is their exclusion from the financial system. This is the fundamental flaw of our conventional formal financial systems. As a result, these households find it extremely difficult to take advantage of economic opportunities, build assets, finance their children's education, and protect themselves against external financial shocks. One can argue that financial exclusion not only pushes them but also tightly binds them into a vicious circle of poverty.

Fortunately, visionary social entrepreneurs like Professor Muhammad Yunus, the pioneer of the Grameen Bank of Bangladesh, have shown the world that financial exclusion is simply unacceptable; its underlying premise that the poor people are not bankable is simply incorrect; and, that there are effective ways to address the exclusion.

The Reality of Financial Exclusion

There are two parts to financial exclusion: One, supply side issues that range from access to a bank account to product gaps like savings, micro-pensions and micro-insurance, etc., backed by a technology-enabled, low-transaction cost mechanism front ended by intermediaries like bank branches, banking correspondents, post office and a variety of other outreach mechanisms that also need to work under a financial literacy umbrella of some sorts. These are well-defined issues with relatively simpler answers and therefore, often get confused as the be-all and end-all of financial inclusion. It is the demand side issues where far more daunting challenges lie.

Financial exclusion forms part of a much wider social exclusion, faced by some groups who lack access to quality essential services such as jobs, housing, education or health care. Societal causes such as ageing combined with the technological gap increase financial exclusion. However, many factors for exclusion are on supply and demand: banks refusing to open full transaction bank accounts for certain groups of people; lack of accessibility, inadequate product design, bad service delivery and high price associated with transaction bank accounts deterring people to access and/or use those services. Belief that bank accounts are not for poor people, concerns about costs or the fear of loss of financial control also play a role. Underpinning financial exclusion are problems of poverty, ignorance and environment:

- Poverty: being on a low income, especially out of work and on benefits.
- Ignorance: low levels of awareness and understanding of products caused by lack of appropriate marketing or low levels of financial literacy.
- Environment: lack of access to financial services caused by several factors, including:
  - geographic access to bank branches or remote banking facilities;
  - affordability of products such as insurance, where premiums often price out those living in the most deprived and risky areas;
  - suitability of products like current accounts, which offer an overdraft and an easy route to debt;
  - cultural and psychological barriers, such as language, caste, perceived/actual racism and suspicion or fear of financial institutions.

There is a large overlap between poverty and permanent financial exclusion. Both poverty and financial exclusion result in a reduction of choices which affects social interaction and leads to reduced participation in society. A major cause of poverty among rural people in India today is the lack of access for both individuals and communities to productive assets and financial resources. High levels of illiteracy, inadequate health care and extremely limited access to social services are common among poor rural people. The financially excluded typically exhibit one or more of the following characteristics:

- Lack of a bank account and the financial services that come with it.
- Reliance on alternative forms of credit, such as doorstep lenders and pawnbrokers.
- Lack of other key financial products, such as insurance, savings products and pensions.
- Lack of capacity and livelihood alternatives.

There exist many such examples which have direct linkage of livelihood with poverty alleviation. One such example is an intervention led by NABARD called Wadi at Vansda, Gujarat. It was a dryland inhabited by tribals and had small holdings of land ranging from one acre to five acres. They had no access to education and had adopted old and traditional ways of farming. With the help of Bharatiya Agro Industries Foundation (BAIF)—a local NGO—these tribals started cashew and mango cultivation and other income generation activities. SHGs were formed and were trained in pot-drip making, digging ponds for watershed, vermicompost making and so on. They were also trained into a habit of thrift and savings. What actually started as an agri-forestry-horticulture development programme has turned out to be a financial inclusion project.[3]

Financial inclusion attained through SHGs is sustainable and scalable on account of its various positive features. One of the distinctive features of the SHG-bank linkage programme has been the high recovery rate. Financial inclusion will undoubtedly result in additional costs, for instance, in extending the outreach to include small borrowers. Capacity building is essential. While part of it can be borne by the banks themselves, a part, particularly that relating to promotional efforts and building capacities, will have to be borne by the government.

Alternatively, it is believed by Haseeb Drabu, Chairman of Jammu & Kashmir Bank and economic adviser to the J&K Government, that while opening a no-frills accounts for everyone makes up for financial inclusion, this is only a definitional, and not an operative or a functional, form of financial inclusion. "The reforms initiated in the early 1990s have attempted to enhance allocative efficiency, not distributive gains. As such, the Reserve Bank of India has made reformist changes only in the structure and development of financial markets, especially the money, government securities and forex markets. Reform of the credit market has been conspicuous by its absence. One is tempted to compare this with the overall economic reforms in general and agricultural reforms in particular that have been carried out without land reform! The moment credit markets are restructured as a part of the overall agenda of financial sector reforms, financial inclusion will get underway in a self-sustaining manner and will not be seen as some kind of corporate social responsibility."[4]

---

3. See Annexure A-2, "Wadi: Planting Hopes", in Kochhar, Sameer, R, Chandrashekhar, K.C. Chakrabarty and Deepak B. Phatak (eds.) (2009). *Financial Inclusion*. New Delhi: Academic Foundation. pp.186-88.
4. Drabu, Haseeb (2008). "Economics and Inclusion", Speech delivered at 17th Skoch Summit 2009, June 2008, Mumbai.

Financial Inclusion needs to be Preceded by Social Inclusion[5]

Inadequate Physical Capital: A vast majority of financially excluded regions suffer from low level of investment in roads, bridges, canals, power supply and market linkages. Absence of these leads to a general malaise in the local economy.[6] A example of how introduction of such facilities changes lifestyles is evident from the Pradhan Mantri Gram Sadak Yojana (PMGSY), which was extensively studied by Skoch during the summer of 2008 at Samotakabas village, Sikar; Khedisuwa and Swamikabas villages in Jaipur in Rajasthan; Umri and Chakur villages in Wardha, Jhanjzorli, Mithaghar and Sarvepada villages in Thane, Maharashtra, in addition to Kalahandi in Orissa and Karauli in Rajasthan. The benefits reported were easier access to markets, better prices for farm produce, faster repair of electrical faults, access to mechanised farming, increase in girls attending schools, improvement in health care services and so on.[7] Further, NREGS has enabled people to get employment and guaranteed wages, which are getting directly transferred to their accounts. Most of these people did not have bank accounts earlier. These projects have played their respective roles in bringing economic enablement and empowerment to the people at the grassroots.

Underdeveloped Social Capital: Gram panchayats, commodity cooperatives, local administration and even local markets in the financially excluded regions are not well developed.[8]

Low Productivity: Regions that have a low degree of financial inclusion, also exhibit a low level of agricultural productivity.[9]

Poor Market Linkages: Particularly true in case of north-eastern states substantial quantities go waste because they cannot be marketed.

5. "Report of the Committee on Financial Inclusion," Economic Advisory Council to the Prime Minister, Government of India, January 2008, p.108.
6. "Report of the Committee on Financial Inclusion," Economic Advisory Council to the Prime Minister, Government of India, January 2008, p.107.
7. Kochhar, Sameer and Gursharan Dhanjal (2008). "Participatory Democracy, Infrastructure and Empowerment", in Sameer Kochhar, Deepak B. Phatak, H. Krishnamurthy and Gursharan Dhanjal (eds.), *Infrastructure & Governance*. New Delhi: Academic Foundation. pp.19-20.
8. Ibid.
9. Ibid.

Development of the local economy with forward and backward market linkages is essential for upliftment of the local economy and rural poor. Ethnic minorities are facing wide-ranging economic and social disadvantages and day-to-day humiliation and degradation and denial of justice.[10]

Low Education: Ethnic minorities have been excluded from the education system.[11] There are many such examples. Out of a few known to us include Van Gujjars, who are the inhabitants of Rajaji National Park in Uttarakhand. This tribal minority community—by virtue of them being nomadic—have apparently not been able to find their place in the national census and have remained excluded for generations. Illiterate as they are, not only do they not have any access to credit, formal or informal, but they are also not exposed to any other sort of financial services. Due to their nomadic nature, their non-stationary existence has made them depend largely on agricultural resources. Another example is the Nishi tribal village called Sangram situated on the Sino-Indian border in remote Arunachal Pradesh. It is a living example of a subsistence economy. With no formal access to education of any sort and the social milieu that is loaded against the girl child, who is bartered for economic benefits, they along with many such others have ever remained excluded from the national mainstream, both socially as well as financially. There exist hundreds of similar stories wherein the conditions of poverty have prevailed more than ever before.

Limited Employment Opportunities: Incidence of landlessness, lack of education and capacity leads to migration and further marginalisation.[12]

Social Discrimination and Political Marginalisation: Factors like high rural households having no bank account and also high share of rural households without specified assets indicate higher incidence of rural unrest and political instability and emergence of Naxalism.[13] Equal access to education for women and girls will be ensured; poverty eradication

10. "Development Challenges in Extremist Affected Areas", Report of an Expert Group to Planning Commission, Government of India, New Delhi, 2008, p.4.

11. Ibid.: 5.

12. Ibid.

13. Ibid.: 20.

programmes will specifically address the needs and problems of such women; women's access to credit for consumption and production will be enhanced.[14]

Experience with Credit Programmes

It was widely believed that the provision of credit for the rural poor results in significant productivity increases. As a consequence, large amounts of money have been channelled to, and through, micro-finance programmes over the past 30–40 years, much of it providing credit for agricultural production. This supply-led approach was based on the premise that credit was an important entry point for promoting development and that advances in other sectors such as health and education would follow naturally.

It is now apparent that access to productive credit (investments in productive activities) cannot alone increase incomes. Individuals and small enterprises also require a conducive economic environment, which creates incentives for production and services, which facilitate market access (including transport infrastructure and market information systems). Supply-led, subsidised credit may lead to inappropriate investments and consequently, indebtedness.

All along, we have seen and experienced first hand that whether it is the Shatabdi Gram Yojana of Bank of India, Integrated Village Development Programme of Bank of Baroda or Micro-Credit scheme of State Bank of India, the involvement of self help groups (SHGs) has proved to be a major catalyst to financial inclusion. Kalahandi in Orissa—tainted as one of the most backward districts in India—had remained untouched by the wave of development until State Bank of India decided to bring it into the banking mainstream. The rural branch of SBI in Farah, Kalahandi, is manned only by one official who opens the office, runs errands, plays manager and teller's role and spends evenings spreading awareness about banking benefits. He has been able to mobilise about 200 women SHGs of about 10 women each, who have inculcated the savings habit, opened bank accounts, taken credit and are involved in income generation activities like

14. "National Initiatives Concerning Poverty Alleviation through Education and Training", National Policy for Empowerment of Women 2001, Ministry of Human Resource Development, Government of India.

bamboo craft, toy-making, fisheries, etc. This was just the beginning. Once known for starvation deaths, pockets in Kalahandi are now embarking on the road to progress and prosperity. There are many such initiatives of SHG mobilisation—early examples being Union Bank of India's Village Knowledge Centres in Neerpara, Kerala; Neemrana, Rajasthan; Jind, Haryana and Sangrur, Punjab by PNB; Chittoor, Andhra Pradesh by Corporation Bank;[15] Bidadi, Karnakata by Canara Bank;[16] Pondicherry by Indian Bank; and so on. We have been there, witnessing progress as we travelled. Today, there are as many as 2.8 million SHGs across the country and these are mostly run by women who were hitherto involved only with daily household chores.

Second, low productivity is only one component of poverty; access to health care, education and political representation represent other dimensions of poverty. Only by adopting a broader, holistic approach will ambitious poverty reduction targets be met.

Third, an initial presumption was that the poor had no other financial service needs apart from productive credit. A deeper understanding of the financial needs of the poor has dispelled this myth. Projects now are less likely to focus narrowly on productive credit; increasingly, they include savings components and occasionally, insurance.

Improving financial access in a way that benefits the poor to the greatest extent requires a strategy for inclusion that goes well beyond credit for poor households. There is need for the 'Credit Plus' approach. Since expanding access remains an important challenge even in developed economies, it is not enough to say that the market will provide. Mobilising savings requires considerable institutional development, and the actual cost of funds can be higher than borrowing. It also requires staff skills and systems that are different than those required by organisations engaged only in lending. Finally, the ability to mobilise savings can depend

15. See Annexure A-3, "Corporation Bank: Branchless Banking", in Sameer Kochhar, R. Chandrashekhar, K.C. Chakrabarty and Deepak B. Phatak (eds.) (2009). *Financial Inclusion*. New Delhi: Academic Foundation. pp.189-90.

16. See Annexure A-1, "Canara Bank: 360 Degree Approach to Inclusion", in Sameer Kochhar, R. Chandrashekhar, K.C. Chakrabarty and Deepak B. Phatak (eds.) (2009). *Financial Inclusion*. New Delhi: Academic Foundation. p.185.

significantly on the macroeconomic conditions and on the regulatory environment.[17]

In addition, India can look at adopting a few strategies like redefining the priority sector, involving rural moneylenders as per the Japanese Sarakin Model, focusing on the emerging rural service sector, planning insurance/pension products for the unorganised sector, etc.

Needs of the Poor

The poor clearly require a range of financial services, such as opportunities to safeguard earned income, or credit to enable them to maintain minimum levels of consumption throughout the year. The rural economies within which the majority of poor people live and work are characterised by numerous small transactions. Although the units of exchange in these 'paise economies' appear small and insignificant to outsiders, they are an essential component of rural households' livelihoods. The extent of financial services demanded by the poor is only now being fully appreciated. Although we do not attempt to debate poverty definitions,[18] it is recognised that the poor are not a homogeneous group, and that they have different needs and levels of access to financial services.

Poverty is a result of low level of assets, coupled with low returns. The poor have very few assets beyond their own labour, which is inevitably spent in tedious, back-breaking, low paid work. They often possess little or no land and also tend to lack education, skills and good health. In addition, the poor have limited access to such public assets as community infrastructure, basic services and government schemes. It is seen that rural poverty is becoming increasingly concentrated among households whose primary source of income is casual labour, both in agriculture as well as the rural non-farm sector.

---

17. UNDESA and UNCDF (2006). *The Blue Book: Building Inclusive Financial Sectors for Development*.

18. Poverty, in India, has been defined by the Planning Commission in terms of the level of per capita consumer expenditure sufficient to provide an average daily intake of 2400 calories per person in rural areas and 2100 calories per person in urban areas, plus a minimal allocation for basic non-food items. In this definition, focus is on material deprivation and poverty has been defined in terms of incomes or level of consumption.

The poor in the urban areas too have the same basic financial service needs such as secured savings, credit and additionally, mechanism to transfer remittances back home like their counterparts in rural areas.[19]

Research shows that poor people value financial services, want more of them, worry when they don't have them, but are often frustrated by them when they do get them.[20] They know that managing money is important, and that managing money well gives them a better chance to manage their lives and livelihoods well. Those lives and livelihoods are complex, diverse, dynamic and vulnerable, and the poor want their financial services to respond by being reliable, convenient, continuous and flexible. They are aware that their most dependable forms of social security are their own money and asset-management skills, so they need a wide range of intermediating terms, from a tiny advance of a few rupees to tide over a current food shortage, through loans for investment opportunities, to long term saving instruments that help them manage retirement, widowhood or disability.

A useful distinction can be made between livelihood promotion and livelihood protection.[21] Promotion is concerned with improving standards of living, principally through increasing productivity and incomes. Protection is essentially social security concerned with maintaining living standards and incomes at a given level, and defending livelihoods against unexpected shocks. Clearly the two concepts are complementary. The promotion of livelihoods will tend to make them more robust and able to withstand shocks, whilst sound protection will lay the basis for livelihood promotion.

Experts agree that one of the critical gaps in the ability of poor households to acquire wealth is the dearth of the right type of financial

---

19. Kelkar, Vijay (2008). "Financial Inclusion for Inclusive Growth," *N.P. Sen Memorial Lecture* at Administrative Staff College of India, Hyderabad, January 13. p.12.

20. Ruthven, Orlanda (2001). "Money Mosaics: Financial Choice and Strategy in a West Delhi Squatter Settlement," University of Manchester Institute for Development Policy and Management, Finance and Development Research Programme Paper 32. Also, Ruthven, Orlanda and Sushil Kumar (2002). "Fine-grain Finance: Financial Choice and Strategy Among the Poor in Rural North India," University of Manchester Institute for Development Policy and Management, Finance and Development Research Programme Paper 57.

21. Dreze, J. and A. Sen (1989). *Hunger and Public Action*. Oxford: Oxford University Press. p. 60.

services—low cost credit, safe ways to save, efficient means to move their cash, emergency relief and the availability of long-term products that can be used for their later years. The Consultative Group to Assist the Poor (CGAP), a donor consortium run by the World Bank, estimates that around three billion people lack basic financial services such as savings accounts and access to credit.

Financial sector reform is a part of development policy and therefore, should focus on creating a broader array of financial services for a broader section of the deprived or underserved population.

Defining Rural Finance

The Consultative Group to Assist the Poor (CGAP) defines rural finance as 'financial services offered and used in rural areas by people of all income levels', and agricultural finance as 'a sub-set of rural finance dedicated to financing agriculture related activities, such as input, supply, production, distribution and wholesaling, and marketing.'

Rural finance encompasses all the savings, lending, financing and risk minimising opportunities (formal and informal) and related norms and institutions in rural areas.

This definition recognises that rural financial markets are part of the domestic financial system and are therefore, affected by government and central bank policies. Rural financial markets tend to be fragmented and consist of formal, semi-formal and informal financial intermediaries. The definition also acknowledges that the rural population requires a range of financial services.

An important question that arises logically is: has commensurate financial deepening been taking place at the micro-level? There is sufficient anecdotal evidence to suggest that the poor or less well-off people find it difficult to open a bank account in any area—rural, urban or semi-urban. Thus, not only is the common individual deprived of access to banks for generating savings or availing credit, but so is the financial system of resources commensurate with the burgeoning growth of incomes all over the country. It is this very feature that the process of financial inclusion seeks to address.[22]

Improvements in financial services, both formal and informal, must be tailored to the needs of the poor. This requires innovative approaches for increased awareness about the benefits and the kind of financial

22. Mohan, Rakesh (2006). "Economic Growth, Financial Deepening and Financial Inclusion", Address at the Annual Bankers, Conference 2006, at Hyderabad on November 3. *http://www.rbi.org.in/scripts/BS_SpeechesView.aspx?Id=310*

services available and finally, their accessibility in remote unbanked areas. In Tineri village in Bihar, PNB is using the *panchayat* as a facilitator for financial literacy. Tineri was visited by us recently to document the change that it has brought to people's lives. The participation levels are high as the people were found to be comfortable in interacting with *panchayat* functionaries and in accepting the information being shared.[23]

Two key strategies are savings mobilisation, and linking the informal and formal sectors. Banks can help mobilise the savings of the poor by removing restrictions on withdrawals from savings accounts and simplifying lending operations and procedures. Credit access programmes should aim to increase women's access to credit within the formal sector, either through direct contact or by linking informal and formal financial activities.

The decentralised/linkage banking model has considerable potential. It seeks to build on the relative strengths of existing formal and informal units. It adopts a holistic approach, which integrates the complementary roles of financial and non-financial public and non-governmental organisations in reducing gaps in the supply of financial services to the poor. Group-based activities, both for savings and credit, can potentially play a significant role in improving access to financial services, as they provide a means for risk-sharing and a reduction of transaction costs.

Attention must be given to the limitations of the poor in making savings and importantly, using credit in productive ways. The impact on incomes tends to be greater when credit is combined with non-financial business development activities. The macroeconomic context is also critical: price stability and fiscal policy are particularly important factors.

Towards an Enabling Environment

Access to financial services helps the poor catch up with the rest of the economy as it grows. But mere access to financial services does not; there has to be a livelihood dimension that goes along with it. Largely thanks to

---

23. See Chakrabarty, K.C. (2009). "The Tineri Experience", in Sameer Kochhar, R. Chandrashekhar, K.C. Chakrabarty and Deepak B. Phatak (eds.) (2009). *Financial Inclusion*. New Delhi: Academic Foundation. pp.53-54. Also see "Window of Opportunity at Tineri," *Inclusion* (Quarterly), October-December 2008, pp.40-41.

microfinance, there is now a growing appreciation of the "empowerment" dimension of finance, of the extent to which it can give ordinary people and the poor access to opportunity and the ability to escape ossified social structures. It is perhaps symbolic of this evolutionary thinking that "building inclusive financial systems that work for the poor" became the *mantra* of the United Nations International Year of Microcredit, 2005. The Year of Microcredit helped dispel the notion that the poor are "irresponsible with money". Indeed, it has confirmed that they are not only "bankable" clients, but a very important and largely untapped financial market. Despite their lack of traditional sources of collateral, micro-entrepreneurs demonstrate that "peer group pressure", as well as self-interest in a lasting source of funds, are usually sufficient to ensure good repayment rates.

Experience and research suggest that demand from poor and low income customers for financial services grows when financial service providers understand what customers use and value, and then offer products and services that customers want to buy. When these providers function with appropriate pricing, with efficient, streamlined institutional structures and with solid risk management systems, they can become profitable business ventures that reach the scale necessary to be significant players within a very large market.

Since the early national plans, successive governments in independent India have rightly emphasised on the link to improving access to finance and reducing poverty. The need to improve financial access for India's poor, the overwhelming majority of whom are concentrated in rural areas, motivated the establishment of a vast network of rural cooperative credit banks in the 1950s, followed by a drive to nationalise commercial banks, launched in 1969. This led to thousands of new bank branches in rural areas across the country.

The strategy during the 1970s and 1980s gave the lead role to the nationalised commercial banks, who were charged with loosening the grip of traditional informal sector moneylenders through the use of targeted low-priced loans.[24] The 1990s saw the partial deregulation of interest rates, increased competition in the banking sector, and new microfinance

24. Reddy, Y.V. (1999). "Future of Rural Banking", *Prof. G. Ram Reddy Third Endowment Lecture*, Hyderabad, India, December 4. Reserve Bank of India, available at *rbidocs.rbi.org.in/rdocs/Bulletin/DOCs/10991.doc*

approaches, most notably, a nationwide attempt, pioneered by non-governmental organisations (NGOs) and now supported by the state, to create links between commercial banks, NGOs and SHGs. The SHG-Bank linkage approach has grown dramatically over the past decade, but its outreach is still modest in terms of the proportion of poor households served. Moreover, informal sector lenders remain a strong presence in rural India, delivering finance to the poor, the vast majority of whom still do not have access to either formal or semi-formal (microfinance) sectors.

There are still under-banked states in the country, such as Bihar, Orissa, Rajasthan, Uttar Pradesh, Chhattisgarh, Jharkhand, West Bengal and a large number of north-eastern states, where the average population per branch office continues to be quite high compared to the national average. The branch authorisation policy of the Reserve Bank of India encourages banks to open branches in these states and in the under-banked areas in other states. The new policy also places a lot of emphasis on the efforts made by the RBI to achieve, *inter alia*, financial inclusion and other policy objectives.[25]

There are several rural and urban poverty alleviation programmes promoted by Government, notably the National Rural Employment Guarantee Programme (NREGA). From April 2008, the NREGA which ensures that every rural household in need can ask for paid wage work up to 100 days per [illegible], was rolled out nationwide. Banks and post offices are being made intermediaries for routing NREGP payments through bank accounts to enhance financial inclusion. There is no denying that the NREGA is a unique and revolutionary social programme, and it is already showing inspirational results. However, very soon what is being given today as a relief measure will tomorrow become a right. Then, the question of sustainability will arise; and, how the government will bank all the requirements. The next round of growth has to come out of poverty alleviation or else the growth itself will not be sustainable. Instead of poverty alleviation, we will end up with poverty perpetuation.

The growing body of research shows that well-developed and inclusive financial systems are associated with more rapid growth and better income

25. Commemorative Lecture by V. Leeladhar, Deputy Governor, Reserve Bank of India at the Fedbank Hormis Memorial Foundation at Ernakulam, December 2, 2005.

distribution. Specifically, financial depth plays a role in lowering inequality and increasing the income of the bottom 80 per cent of the population. Further, a seminal study into India's banking system found that the rural bank expansion programme, mandated by the Indian government from 1977–1990, helped to explain approximately half of the drop in poverty from 61 per cent in 1967 to 31 per cent in 2000 (Burgess and Pande, 2003).[26]

Financial inclusion has to be viewed as a business strategy for growth: a) Enhanced financial inclusion will reduce the farmers' indebtedness; b) Enhanced financial inclusion means better risk management tools for the farmers, they will be encouraged to adopt new technologies at a faster rate; c) By providing greater access to educational loans to all sections of society, improved financial inclusion will mean India becoming more equal opportunity nation, a pre-condition for promoting inclusive growth; and, d) Enhanced financial inclusion will promote grassroots innovations and entrepreneurship.[27]

India's stable political environment and strong economic growth over the last 10 years has put the country in a position to become the third largest economy in the world by 2050. At the same time, India accounts for the largest share of the world's poor and its economic development is characterised by a widening income gap between the rich and the poor. The increasingly favourable economic climate in India presents a great opportunity to speed up financial inclusion initiatives and alleviate poverty on a large scale.

Scaling-up access to finance for India's rural poor, to meet their diverse financial needs (savings, credit, insurance, etc.) through flexible products at competitive prices, presents a formidable developmental challenge in a country as vast and varied as India. But the opportunities too are plentiful, and the government has an important role to play in creating space and a flexible architecture for innovations. Financial inclusion is, and needs to be seen as, crucial in achieving pro-poor growth and poverty reduction goals.

---

26. Quoted in Ramji, Minakshi (2009). "Financial Inclusion in Gulbarga: Finding Usage Through Access". Paper presented at CAB Conference on *Microfinance: From Research to Practice*, Pune, January 16-17.

27. Kelkar, Vijay (2008). "Financial Inclusion for Inclusive Growth," N.P. Sen Memorial Lecture at Administrative Staff College of India, Hyderabad, January 13, pp. 13-14.

3 Setting the Stage for Financial Inclusion

In its landmark research work titled *Building Inclusive Financial Sectors for Development*,[1] the United Nations raised a basic question "Why are so many bankable people unbanked?" Financial inclusion has become an issue which is at the centrestage of all international and national deliberations, in the context of formulating development strategies that touch the lives of the economically weaker segments of the population, to increase their participation in the process of economic growth and social development. It involves the all-important process of ensuring access to a range of financial services such as bank accounts, credit, remittances and payments, insurance facilities and financial advisory services, at an affordable cost to the economically vulnerable groups. The banking sector in India has recognised this imperative and has undergone fundamental changes in the last two decades.

Bank nationalisation in India marked a paradigm shift in the focus of banking as it was intended to shift the focus from class banking to mass banking. The rationale for creating regional rural banks (RRBs) was also to take the banking services to poor people. The branches of commercial banks and the RRBs have increased from 8,321 in the year 1969 to 68,282 branches as at the end of March 2005. The average population per branch office has decreased from 64,000 to 16,000 during the same period. However, there are certain under-banked states such as Bihar, Orissa, Rajasthan, Uttar Pradesh, Chhattisgarh, Jharkhand, West Bengal and a large number of north-eastern states, where the average population per branch office continues to be quite high compared to the national average. The new branch authorisation policy of Reserve Bank encourages banks to open branches in these under-banked states and the under-banked areas in other states.

---

1. UNDESA and UNCDF (2006). *The Blue Book: Building Inclusive Financial Sectors for Development.*

The focus on rural banking arises from the fact that poverty in India is extremely well-entrenched in rural areas, with over 70 per cent of India's poor residing in its villages.[2] While the area and population served per rural bank branch in India compares favourably with other developing nations, an overwhelming majority of small and marginal farmers do not have access to savings or credit account.[3] As such while India's system can be said to be financially deep in terms of access, it would appear that it scores poorly on translating this into usage. Rural households face several barriers when they attempt to borrow from banks.[4] Firstly, banks demand collateral which poor people are unable to provide. Secondly, bank transactions tend to be time-consuming and expensive. Bribes amounting to 20 per cent of the loan amount are not unheard of. Furthermore, on average, bank loans take 33 weeks to be approved. Consequently, the share of informal sources of credit (moneylenders, pawnbrokers, friends and family) has jumped to 27 per cent in 2002 from 17.5 per cent in 1991.[5]

The focus on credit has meant that policy and practice has thus far ignored the provision of a safe place for savings for rural households,[6] in spite of evidence that poor people do save. India has approximately 300 million savings accounts which would imply that about 59 per cent of India's adult population has access to a savings account.[7] Since public policy responses to cope with lack of financial services access have typically used savings banks to increase access, a strong and stable savings bank system can be important to achieve universal access. The drive for financial inclusion, initiated by the RBI and described below, is thus significant in that it attempts to extend savings bank accounts to 'unbanked' households.

---

2. Basu, Priya (2005). "A Financial System for India's Poor", *Economic and Political Weekly*. September 10, pp.4008-4012.
3. Basu, Priya (2006). *Improving Access to Finance for India's Rural Poor.* Washington D.C.: The World Bank.
4. N. 2.
5. Mohan, Rakesh (2006). "Economic Growth, Financial Deepening and Financial Inclusion", Address at the Annual Bankers' Conference, Hyderabad, November 3.
6. Ghate, Prabhu (2007). "Consumer Protection in India Microfinance: Lessons from Andhra Pradesh and the Microfinance Bill", *Economic and Political Weekly*, March 31.
7. Leeladhar, V. (2005). *Taking Banking Services to the Common Man Financial Inclusion*. Ernakulam: Fedbank Hormis Memorial Foundation. December 2.

Despite the depth of the Indian financial system, and the country's wide network of rural banks, India's poor households, who are concentrated in rural areas, still have very little access to formal finance. A World Bank-NCAER Survey on rural access to finance (the Rural Finance Access Survey-RFAS, 2003) indicates that 70 per cent of the rural poor do not have a bank account and 87 per cent have no access to credit from a formal source. Informal sector lenders remain a strong presence in rural India, delivering finance to the poor: the RFAS, 2003 finds that 48 per cent of landless and marginal farmers borrowed from an informal source at least once in the past 12 months, at rates averaging 48 per cent per year.[8]

Another study by Diamond Management and Technology Consultants concluded that less than 20 per cent of rural Indians have access to formal financial services, and about 185 million "potentially bankable" people in rural India do not have a bank account.[9] However, the problem of access to finance is not confined to rural areas. According to the Banking Ombudsman of Karnataka state, 63 per cent of the people in the country do not have the benefit of banking facilities.[10] The financially excluded sections largely comprise marginal farmers, landless labourers, self-employed and unorganised sector enterprises, urban slum dwellers, ethnic minorities, migrants and women. Most of the excluded people are concentrated in the north eastern, eastern and central regions.[11]

One of the benchmarks employed to assess the degree of reach of financial services to the population of the country, is the quantum of deposit accounts (current and savings) held as a ratio to the adult population. In the Indian context, taking into account the Census of 2001 (ignoring the incremental growth of population thereafter), the ratio of deposit accounts (data available as on March 31, 2004) to the total adult population was only 59 per cent. Within the country, there is a wide variation across states. For instance, the ratio for the state of Kerala is

8. Basu, Priya and Pradeep Srivastava (2004). *Scaling-up Access to Finance for India's Rural Poor*.

9. Diamond Management and Technology Consultants (2006). *Building a More Inclusive Financial System in India*. Mumbai: DMTC.

10. "Promote No-frills Accounts", *Hindu Business Line*. September 26, 2006.

11. Thorat, Usha (2007). "Financial Inclusion–The Indian Experience", Speech made at the *HMT-DFID Financial Inclusion Conference*. London, June 19, available at *www.rbi.org.in/scripts/speeches*

as high as 89 per cent while Bihar is marked by a low coverage of 33 per cent. In the north eastern states like Nagaland and Manipur, the coverage was a meagre 21 per cent and 27 per cent, respectively. The northern region, comprising the states of Haryana, Chandigarh and Delhi, has a high coverage ratio of 84 per cent. Compared to the developed world, the coverage of our financial services is quite low. In the first-ever Index of Financial Inclusion[12] to find out the extent of reach of banking services among 100 countries, India has been ranked 50. Only 34 per cent Indian individuals have access to or receive banking services.

In the context of initiatives taken for extending banking services to the small man, the mode of financial sector development until 1980s was characterised by:

- a hugely expanded bank branch and cooperative network and new organisational forms like RRBs;
- a greater focus on credit rather than other financial services like savings and insurance, although the banks and cooperatives did provide deposit facilities;
- lending targets directed at a range of 'priority sectors' such as agriculture, weaker sections of the population, etc;
- interest rate ceilings;
- significant government subsidies channelled through the banks and cooperatives, as well as through related government programmes;
- a dominant perspective that finance for rural and poor people was a social obligation and not a potential business opportunity.

It is absolutely beyond any doubt that the financial access to masses has significantly improved in the last three and a half decades. But the basic question is, has that been good enough? The quantum of deposit accounts (current and savings) held as a ratio to the adult population has not been uniformly encouraging. There is a tremendous scope for financial coverage if we have to improve the standard of living of the poor and marginalised.

---

12. Sarma, Mandira (2008). "Index of Financial Inclusion", *ICRIER Working Paper* No. 215. New Delhi: ICRIER.

Role of Microfinance

Microfinance has been long recognised and practised in India as a tool for extending banking services to the poor to enable them to save and invest or partake of credit, thereby facilitating them to break the chain of poverty. Several micro-credit schemes have brought rich rewards to the beneficiaries. With hardly any non-performing asset (NPAs) in micro-credit, more and more banks are looking at increasing their operations in this area in a big way.

The self help group (SHG) which provides a good bank linkage programme, is a major plank of the strategy for delivering financial services to the poor in a sustainable manner. As at the end of March 2007, as many as 2.92 million SHGs have been credit linked with banks, benefitting more than 40 million poor families; 80 per cent of members of self help groups constitute women.

But microfinance still plays a modest role in India. At all-India level, less than 5 per cent of poor rural households have access to microfinance (as compared to 65 per cent in Bangladesh) but significant variations exist across states. The southern states in particular, account for almost 75 per cent of funds flowing under microfinance programmes. By far the most successful model of microfinance in India, in terms of scale and outreach, is SHG-Bank linkage, with other models, such as the 'Grameen-type' independent microfinance institutions, lagging far behind.[13]

Today, most microfinance industry clients are very near the poverty line. Yet, one of the biggest challenges facing the microfinance industry today is developing financial products and methodologies for very poor or difficult-to-reach rural populations, reducing their vulnerability and increasing their economic well-being. An extensive impact study undertaken across 20 NGO-MFIs operating in different parts of India found that, typically only 35 per cent of MFI clients in the country can strictly be classified as poor.[14]

---

13. Basu, Priya and Pradeep Srivastava (2004). *Scaling-up Access to Finance for India's Rural Poor.*

14. EDA Rural Systems Private Limited (2004) *The Maturing of Indian Microfinance: An Impact Assessment of 20 MFIs*. Sponsored by SIDBI. EDA Rural Systems Private Limited, Gurgaon, India.

The industry has not as yet paid adequate attention to pushing the frontier of services to include the poorest. In most countries, microfinance does not reach many remote areas or poorer states or provinces. In India, most outreach is concentrated in three or four southern states, while states with a much higher poverty incidence have not benefited from the industry's growth. With few exceptions, microfinance is heavily credit biased. Demand-driven deposit services, micro-insurance and domestic money transfer services are yet to become a major component of the industry's scope of services.

First, we must recognise the pivotal need to bring down the high cost of semi-formal and formal microfinance. For example, some institutions in the region, charge effective annual interest rates in the range of 40 per cent to 80 per cent on microcredit. Many poor people borrow at these rates because the alternative source of credit for such people is the informal markets where the rates are much higher and usurious. We also need to recognise that there are many millions of poor people who are unable to access the services of semi-formal and formal sources, partly because the prices charged on the products and services are high and beyond their ability to pay.

While charging cost recovery interest rates is important for financial viability, profit and growth of the institutions, it is also essential to improve efficiency and reduce costs so that interest rates do not have to be exorbitant.

Adequate attention has not been paid to the importance of improving efficiency and reducing high costs in the industry. The answer to high costs and high interest rates, however, is neither subsidies nor interest rate caps on loans to the poor because both would reduce, rather increase, poor people's access to financial services, and thereby eventually hurt them. Efforts to promote microfinance should go hand-in-hand with efforts to make the formal sector better at "banking the poor", and government can play a critical role in this context, too.[15]

Importantly, financial inclusion needs to be looked at from both a demand and supply side perspective. Here we examine the demand-side factors. Supply side factors are discussed in Chapter 6.

---

15. Basu, Priya and Pradeep Srivastava (2004). *Scaling-up Access to Finance for India's Rural Poor.*

Steps Towards Financial Inclusion: Demand Side

Demand side issues relating to financial inclusion can be looked at in two ways:

- To extend banking facilities in untapped/non-banked areas.
- To extend innovative and affordable microfinance services for those who lack access to financial services.

To address the issue of financial exclusion in a holistic manner, it is essential to ensure that a range of financial services is available to every individual. These services are:

(i) a no-frills banking account for making and receiving payments,

(ii) a savings product suited to the pattern of cash flows of a poor household,

(iii) money transfer facilities,

(iv) small loans and overdrafts for productive, personal and other purposes,

(v) micro-insurance (life and non-life), ideally combination products, and

(vi) micro-pensions.

The focus of recent policy initiatives has been to promote financial inclusion by merely providing basic banking services to the common person. The broad approach to financial inclusion (demand side) should primarily aim at 'connecting people' with the banking system and credit dispensation; giving people access to payment systems; and articulating financial inclusion as a viable business model and opportunity.

In order to address the issues of financial inclusion, the Government of India constituted a "Committee on Financial Inclusion" under the Chairmanship of Dr. C. Rangarajan. The Committee submitted its final report to the Union Finance Minister on January 4, 2008.

Committee on Financial Inclusion

The Rangarajan Committee has defined financial inclusion as "the process of ensuring access to financial services and timely and adequate credit where needed by vulnerable groups such as weaker sections and low income groups at an affordable cost."[16]

The Committee observed that in India, 51.4 per cent of farmer households are financially excluded from both formal and informal sources and 73 per cent of the farmer households do not access formal sources of credit. Those excluded are mostly marginal farmers and women.

Per cent of Financial Exclusion	States
> 75 per cent	Meghalaya, Mizoram, Jharkhand, Uttarakhand, Arunachal Pradesh, Assam, Manipur
51–75 per cent	Bihar, Orissa, Chhattisgarh, Himachal Pradesh, Jammu and Kashmir, Uttar Pradesh, Nagaland, Tripura, Sikkim
25–50 per cent	Karnataka, Kerala, Madhya Pradesh, Maharashtra, Punjab, Tamil Nadu, West Bengal, Rajasthan
< 25 per cent	Andhra Pradesh, Delhi, Goa, Pondicherry

Inclusive finance—through secure savings, appropriately priced credit and insurance products, and payment services—helps vulnerable groups such as low income groups, weaker sections, etc., to increase incomes, acquire capital, manage risk and work their way out of poverty, noted the Committee report.[17]

The major recommendations of the Committee include:

(i) Launching of a National Rural Financial Inclusion Plan (NRFIP) in mission mode with a clear target to provide access to comprehensive financial services, including credit, to at least 50 per cent (say 55.77 million) of the financially excluded rural cultivator/non-cultivator households, by 2012 through rural/semi-urban branches of commercial banks and regional rural banks. The remaining households have to be covered by 2015. For this purpose, a National Mission on Financial Inclusion (NaMFI) is proposed to be constituted comprising representatives from all stakeholders to aim at achieving universal financial inclusion within a specific time frame.

---

16. "Report of the Committee on Financial Inclusion," Economic Advisory Council to the Prime Minister, Government of India, January 2008, p.1.

17. "Report of the Rangarajan Committee on Financial Inclusion," Economic Advisory Council to the Prime Minister, Government of India, January 2008, p.i, p.28.

(ii) Constitution of two funds with NABARD—the Financial Inclusion Promotion & Development Fund (FIPF) and the Financial Inclusion Technology Fund(FITF) with an initial corpus of Rs. 500 crore each to be contributed by GoI/RBI/NABARD. The FIPF will focus on interventions like, "Farmers' Service Centres", "Promoting Rural Entrepreneurship", "Self-Help Groups and their Federations", "Developing Human Resources of Banks", "Promotion of Resource Centres" and "Capacity Building of Business Facilitators and Correspondents", while the FITF will focus on funding of low-cost technology solutions.

(iii) Deepening the outreach of microfinance programme through financing of SHGs/JLGs and setting up of a risk mitigation mechanism for lending to small marginal farmers/share croppers/ tenant farmers through joint liability groups (JLGs).

(iv) Use of PACSs as business facilitators and correspondents.

(v) Micro Finance—Non Banking Finance Companies (MF-NBFCs) could be permitted to provide thrift, credit, micro-insurance, remittances and other financial services up to a specified amount to the poor in rural, semi-urban and urban areas. Such MF-NBFCs may also be recognised as business correspondents of banks for providing only savings and remittance services and also act as micro insurance agents.

(vi) Opening of specialised microfinance branches/cells in potential urban centres for exclusively catering to microfinance and SHG-Bank linkage requirements of the urban poor. An enabling provision should be made in the NABARD Act, 1981 permitting NABARD to provide microfinance services to the urban poor.

Accordingly, a goal for providing access to financial services to 50 per cent (55.77 million) of the excluded rural cultivator and non-cultivator households across different states by the year 2012 and cent per cent coverage (111.55 million) by the year 2015, has been stipulated.

RBI Takes the Lead

With a view to enhancing the financial inclusion, as a proactive measure, the RBI in its Annual Policy Statement for the year 2005-06, while recognising the concerns in regard to the banking practices that tend to exclude rather than attract vast sections of population, urged banks to review their existing practices to align them with the objective of financial inclusion. In the Mid Term Review of the Policy (2005-06), RBI exhorted the banks, with a view to achieving greater financial inclusion, to make available a basic banking 'no-frills' account either with nil or very minimum balances as well as charges that would make such accounts accessible to vast sections of the population. The nature and number of transactions in such accounts would be restricted and made known to customers in advance in a transparent manner. All banks are urged to give wide publicity to the facility of such no-frills account so as to ensure greater financial inclusion.

Further, in order to ensure that persons belonging to low income group both in urban and rural areas do not face difficulty in opening the bank accounts due to the procedural hassles, the KYC procedure for opening accounts has been simplified for those persons who intend to keep balances not exceeding rupees fifty thousand (Rs. 50,000) in all their accounts taken together and the total credit is not expected to exceed rupees one lakh (Rs.1,00,000) in a year.

Initially, the focus of the financial inclusion was confined to ensuring a bare minimum access to a savings bank account without frills, to all. Internationally, the financial exclusion has been viewed in a much wider perspective. Having a current account/savings account on its own, is not regarded as an accurate indicator of financial inclusion. There could be multiple levels of financial inclusion and exclusion. At one extreme, it is possible to identify the 'super-included', i.e., those customers who are actively and persistently courted by the financial services industry, and who have at their disposal a wide range of financial services and products. At the other extreme, we may have the financially excluded, who are denied access to even the most basic of financial products. In between are those who use the banking services only for deposits and withdrawals of money. But these persons may have only restricted access to the financial system, and may not enjoy the flexibility of access offered to more affluent customers.

The Reserve Bank's broad approach to financial inclusion is:

- Aim at 'connecting' people with the banking system and not just credit dispensation.
- Aim at giving people access to the payments system.
- Use multiple channels such as civil service organisations, NGOs, post offices, farmers' clubs, *panchayats*, MFIs, etc., to expand the outreach of banks.
- Adopt a decentralised approach, which is state and region specific and has close involvement and cooperation between the respective state governments and banks.
- Make use of ICT using biometric smart cards and mobile hand held electronic devices for receipts and disbursement of cash by agents of banks, such as business facilitators/correspondents.
- Portray financial inclusion as a viable business model and opportunity.
- Aim at continuous evaluation, sharing of experiences, feedback and improvement

The RBI understands that the present low level of access to the formal settlement system is a case of market failure and sees its role as trying to "create enabling conditions such that markets become more open, more competitive, affordable and inclusive."[18] Yet, the model, sought to address the problem, continues to emphasise on a bank-based model.

Consequently, while the RBI recognises that there are strong issues on both the demand and supply sides, on demand concerns, it sees geographical barriers, low awareness, low incomes, illiteracy etc., as constraints and on the supply side, branch timings, distance, unfriendly staff, documentation hassles, etc., as problems to circumvent, as these result in high transaction cost. So the RBI has been now looking at solutions such as no-frills account, banking correspondents, use of intermediaries in NGOs, branchless banking, etc.[19]

---

18. Thorat, Usha (2007). "Financial Inclusion – The Indian experience", Speech on June 19.
19. "Financial Inclusion Still Poor in Many Districts", *The Hindu Business Line*, January 27, 2009.

Yet, the importance of financial inclusion becomes important, particularly in the context of doubling the agricultural productivity, targeted for India's 11th Five Year Plan. The RBI report on "Trends and Progress of Banking in India 2007" clearly admits that the progress of microfinance movement in the country has been skewed and the record of financial inclusion has not been up to the mark. Consequently, the RBI has moved to enforce multiple policy and industry changes.

In order to sustain the momentum for financial inclusion, RBI in January 2009 has advised banks to ensure that steps are taken to provide banking services nearer to the location of the no-frills account holders through a variety of channels including satellite offices, mobile offices, business correspondents, etc.

The RBI asked banks to consider providing General Credit Card (GCC)/small overdrafts, along with no-frills accounts, and encourage account holders to actively operate the accounts. Banks should also conduct awareness drives so that the no-frills account holders are made aware of the facilities offered.

The central bank wants banks to efficiently leverage technology enabled financial inclusion initiatives such as smart cards with biometric access involving handheld devices/mobile phones being implemented in various states with its (RBI) support. The RBI has relaxed the norms for mobile banking by raising the caps on fund transfers as well as mobile based payments. Continuing with its earlier announced draft guidelines for mobile banking services in India, RBI has increased fund-transfer limit from Rs. 2,500 a day to Rs. 5,000 a day. The regulator has also provided a cap of Rs. 10,000 for purchases through mobile.[20] The specific focus on security is very welcome and the changes made to the transaction limits moving towards only daily limits will allow more flexibility to the customers for their payments as well as the banks for defining their risk parameters. The move was made after requests from banks to raise the limits for mobile banking transactions.

The apex bank also wants banks to review the extent of coverage in the districts, declared as 100 per cent financially included, in order

20. "Issuance and Operation of Pre-paid Payment Instruments in India (Reserve Bank) Directions, 2009", RBI Circular, April 27, 2009.

to bridge the gaps in banking facilities. RBI's directive to banks comes in the wake of the evaluation of external agencies—Mahatma Gandhi Labour Institute (Ahmedabad), National Institute of Rural Development (Hyderabad), Nabard Consulting Services (Mumbai), Panjab University (Chandigarh), Jadavpur University (Kolkata) and Institute of Development Studies (Jaipur)—regarding 100 per cent financial inclusion in 26 districts of Andhra Pradesh, Gujarat, Himachal Pradesh, Karnataka, Orissa, Punjab, Rajasthan and West Bengal. The findings of these external agencies reveal that most of the accounts opened, as part of banks' financial inclusion drive, have remained inoperative due to various reasons.

The Next Steps?

There are a number of reasons why financial inclusion is not taking place at the desired pace in India. These include coverage, cost of small value transactions, infrastructure, suitable products, flexibility, weak delivery model for community enterprise and financial management support.

With the automation of core banking processes and the use of channels such as ATM, IVR based tele-banking, Internet banking, the banking industry has become lean and more profitable. Banks however, face an uphill task in reaching out to the mass customers in remote locations such as villages. Infrastructure cost, operating expenses, security, understanding of customer behaviour and risk associated with it, and low and slow Return-On-Investment (ROI) inhibit banks from expanding into the rural market.

Rural banking requires extremely ubiquitous technology, that which has an innovative Geographical User Interface (GUI) to deliver an easy user experience. The use of IT solutions for providing banking facilities at doorstep holds the potential for scalability of the FI initiatives. Pilot projects have been initiated using smart cards for opening bank accounts with biometric identification. Link to mobile or handheld connectivity devices ensure that the transactions are recorded in the bank's books on real time basis.

As at the end of December 2008, out of 342 districts identified for 100 per cent FI, 158 districts have reported having achieved 100 per cent FI i.e., all households desirous of opening a bank account have been able to do so. However, the external evaluation studies recently conducted by RBI have revealed that in many cases, these accounts, after having been opened, have not been operated upon, mainly because of the distance to the branch where such account is opened. The distance factor has also inhibited the use of bank accounts for distribution of Government payments such as under the NREGA.[21]

There is increasing recognition that, the spread of literacy and generation of growth impulses in the rural sector would be very significant factors in enhancing effective supply and reducing true cost of rural credit. More specifically, the desired spread of technology and trickledown of urban financial products to rural areas would require concerted action in four areas. First and foremost, insurance, especially of crops, should penetrate the rural areas to mitigate the risks to both farmer and lender. The lack of penetration of insurance is perhaps an important reason for lenders seeking tied and other risk-mitigation arrangements through informal markets. Second, there should be an assured supply of electric power so that functioning of systems is not disrupted. Third, telecommunication network needs to be dependable and financial sector needs to ensure a network. Fourth, the institutional and regulatory framework should enable rural financial institutions to operate in diverse financial products and services.[22]

The global experience on improving access to finance for larger numbers of the population suggests that there is no universally applicable model. As noted by the Rangarajan Committee, financial inclusion can be substantially enhanced by improving the supply side or delivery systems. In order to improve their level of inclusion, demand side efforts need to be undertaken including improving human and physical resources endowments, enhancing productivity, mitigating risk and strengthening market linkages.[23]

---

21. *Draft Report of the High Level Committee to Review the Lead Bank Scheme*. Reserve Bank of India, May 2009, available at *http://rbi.org.in/scripts/PublicationReportDetails.aspx?ID=552* (accessed June 8, 2009).

22. Reddy, Y.V. (1999). *Prof. G. Ram Reddy Third Endowment Lecture*, Potti Sreeramulu Telugu University Auditorium Public Gardens, Hyderabad, December 4.

23. "Report of the Committee on Financial Inclusion," Economic Advisory Council to the Prime Minister, Government of India, January 2008, p.i.

4 What is the Cost of Financial Access?

In early 2006, the RBI came out with a circular, permitting the use of "business correspondents" by bank branches, in order to increase client coverage and financial inclusion. The business correspondents (BCs) would, on behalf of the banks, for a commission, disburse small value credit, recover principal and interest, collect small deposits, receive and deliver small value remittances, and sell micro-insurance, pension and other products.

According to the Rangarajan Committee on Financial Inclusion, reporting a couple of years later, only 27 per cent of farm households have access to bank credit. The committee called for access to financial services, including credit, to be raised to 50 per cent by 2012 (55.77 million households) and 100 per cent by 2015 (111.55 million households). The business correspondent model, riding on appropriate technology, was to be the "core of the strategy", with the goal of having at least one BC in every village.

Hoping to reach unbanked populations, in 2006 RBI encouraged banks to make basic no-frills savings accounts, either with nil or minimum balances, widely available. By December 2008, of the 342 districts identified by State Level Bankers Committee, 158 districts were declared to have achieved 100 per cent financial inclusion, and by the end of March 2008, 15,788,919 no-frills accounts had been opened (according to an RBI 2008 progress report).

As per data collated by the research team, the total number of no-frill accounts opened over a two-year period (April 1, 2007 to May 30, 2009) stands at 25.1 million after discounting those opened under MFI, Rashtriya Swasthya Bima Yojana (RSBY), Bhamasha, etc. The total number of BC IT-enabled accounts is 10.75 million (including inactive accounts) (Table 4.1).

Table 4.1

Number of No-Frill Accounts
(Data From April 1, 2007 to May 30, 2009)

	No-frills Accounts (in Mn)	*Points of Presence*
Technology Provider Enabled No-frill Accounts ^	10.752	13077
Estimated Direct Accounts Opened by Banks Net of 2.5 Mn of Bhamasha Project	18	
Total No-frill Accounts Net of MFI, RSBY and Bhamasha	25.15	
Estimated Number of Operational Accounts out of the Above (11 per cent)	2.77	
Credit/Over Draft in the Above	negligible	
Total Number of Rural Households Targeted for Financial Inclusion##	111.55	

Note: ## Report of the Committee on Financial Inclusion, January 2008.
^ Out of these, 4.4 mn accounts and 7250 points of presence are in Andhra Pradesh.

The starting point of the entire exercise was access to credit for poor, rural households. This does not seem to have incrementally improved at all due to FI initiatives.

Our research meetings revealed that many of these accounts were actually inoperative. But different numbers emerged. Perusal of sample accounts in Cuddalore district in Tamil Nadu, one of the 155 districts declared to be in 100 per cent financially included, revealed that 72 per cent of the accounts had zero or minimum balance even after one year of opening. Only 15 per cent of the accounts had a balance of more than Rs. 100, leaving 85 per cent of the new no-frills accounts inoperative.[1]

Evaluation by external agencies appointed by RBI has also shown that while the first stage of opening no-frills accounts has been quite impressive, due to inadequate follow up, cost of transaction and access constraints, in many cases the accounts have not been operated upon at all after being opened. In order to improve access and use of these accounts, banks will have to offer the services much closer to the customer either

1. The study conducted by S. Thyagarajan at CAB and Jayaram Venkatesan at CMF analysed the results of the financial inclusion project in terms of coverage by geography, account activity and usage and cost involved in opening of accounts and maintenance, as well as the transactional usage behaviour.

through mobile branches, satellite offices, extension counters or using intermediaries like SHGs/MFIs or through business correspondents using IT to increase scale, access and reduce cost. Also as is obvious from the results of these recent studies and surveys, the credit product that has to be offered, if the low-income borrowers have to be brought into the formal system, has to be simple covering all the needs of small borrowers.[2]

We studied 28 pilots as one data set and 1 scale (BC) in Andhra Pradesh as another (see also Table 4.2). About 25 per cent of accounts were active across the 28 pilots largely because of a concentrated effort to make a pilot successful. The AP data reveals that once scaled, only 9.5 per cent of no-frill accounts are active. This is more representative of the real picture as outreach increases. On the basis of informed analysis, we have taken 11 per cent as operational or live accounts. This translates to just 2.77 million live accounts.

So the number of no-frill accounts mistakenly reflects a 25 per cent achievement of the targeted 111.55 million households; the actual in terms of active accounts is only 2.48 per cent more households with bank accounts which they use (minimum of one deposit and one withdrawal per annum).

The reported numbers tend to get distorted to make the technology providers appear as attractive investment propositions. Hence, the phenomenon of carry forward of ongoing inventory of inoperative accounts. One concerted effort was done in Bhamasha where 2.5 million women BPL accounts were to be created. This was done through the Punjab National Bank, and the bank was in the process of hiring 13,000 business correspondents across the state, each equipped with the Rs. 20,000 set of phone/scanner/printer. To incentivise these poor households, the state promised to credit Rs. 1,500 to each family's account. The scheme, powered through a smart card, also promised life and health insurance to the card-holders. Due to elections and change of government in the Rajasthan, the project today, is in limbo.

---

2. Thorat, Usha (2008). Keynote address on "Financial Inclusion and Information Technology" at *Vision 2020-Indian Financial Services Sector*. Mumbai, September 12.

The key point is that of the 10.752 million BC opened accounts, 4.4 million are in Andhra Pradesh alone. Similarly, of the 13,077 points of presence established by BCs, 55.4 per cent (7,250) are in Andhra Pradesh. So, it would not be wrong to assume that financial inclusion seems to be happening largely in one state. In the other states, there just isn't a compelling business case. Andhra Pradesh is the only state government paying a 2 per cent transaction fee on EBT, of which 1.75 per cent goes to the BC and 0.25 per cent to the bank. The RBI has requested other states to emulate the AP model, but there are few takers.

This explains the unwillingness of commercial banks to do financial inclusion. Costs for banks in the BC model have been calculated in Table 4.2 for the two data sets. Calculation of direct costs for the bank (i.e., if the bank itself were to open no-frill accounts) was not undertaken as the extent of outreach envisaged is simply not possible and viable. Direct costs take into account existing investment and infrastructure and not the additional capacity created. In the existing capacity, the cost of transaction is lower simply because of the volumes. A rural branch of SBI handles Rs. 300 million per year (stock and flow combined) while a semi-rural branch handles Rs. 450 million per year (stock and flow combined). A BC point of presence currently disburses Rs. 1.2 million per annum.

The accounts in Andhra Pradesh comprised 30 per cent pension accounts and 70 per cent NREGA accounts, therefore, the usage pattern is higher (2.43) despite the lower percentage of active accounts when compared to pilots (1.42).

Smart card based payouts seem to have now stabilised at Rs. 145 per account for Year 1 (Rs. 80 technology cost+Rs. 65 servicing cost) and Rs. 65 for Year 2 (See also Table 4.3.). In AP, however, the BC is using plastic card largely as proof of photo ID, so the technology and account servicing cost is much lower at Rs. 30.94. (It is further to be noted that in AP, the BC is paid servicing charges only for active accounts unlike in the smart-card based pilots.)

It is widely assumed that the bank carries no cost in the BC model. That is not the case. It is still incurring training, administrative, back office technology and cash management costs, which amounts to Rs. 12.97 per account per year and Rs. 25.94 over two years (Table 4.4). In a scale rollout (e.g. Andhra Pradesh), this cost is likely to go down by 50 per cent. However, if we add this cost to the BC payout, we get a total cost of Rs. 235.94 per smart card account, whereas the cost for plastic card account totals to Rs. 45.82.

Table 4.2

Cost of No-Frill Accounts

Over 2 Years (April 1, 2007 to May 30, 2009)	*Smart Card Based Pilot Projects Covering 28 Lcations*	*Scale Roll-out in Andhra Pradesh using Plastic Cards*
Number of BC Operated No-frill Accounts	150000	2930000
Number of Active Accounts	37500	278350
Average No. of Transactions Per Account -Yr1+Yr2	1.42	2.432
Average No. of Transactions Per Live Account -Yr1 + Yr2	5.30	25.60
Technology + BC Payout Per Account- Yr1 + Yr2 I	210	30.944
Back End Cost Per Account – Yr1+Yr2 II**	25.94	14.88
Cost Per Account Yr1+Yr2 I + II#	235.94	45.82
Technology + BC Payout Per Live Account III	840.00	326.73
Back End Cost Per Live Account D.	103.76	156.63
Cost Per Live Account - III + D	943.76	483.37
Per Transaction Cost (Technology +BC) A.	147.89	12.72
Back End Cost Per Transaction B.	18.27	6.12
Total Per Transaction Cost A+B	166.15	18.84
Per Transaction Cost (Technology +BC) Live Account C.	158.49	12.97
Total Per Transaction Cost—Live Account C+D	262.25	169.60

Note: ** Derived from Table 4.4.
Refer Table 4.5.

The costs rise considerably if we compute the same on the basis of live accounts (25 per cent in the smart card pilots and 9.5 per cent in plastic card scale rollout). The corresponding figure is Rs. 943.76 for smart card accounts and Rs. 483.37 for plastic card accounts.

As an aside, if an account is being opened to service NREGA payments alone, under which the maximum benefit transfer for 100 days of work is Rs. 7,000 per year,[3] using the smart card model the cost of

3. The 2009-10 Budget has raised this to Rs. 100 per day, a total of Rs. 10,000 in a year for 100 days work per family.

reaching the payment is 6.7 per cent and 3.4 per cent using plastic card. The transaction fee, currently being paid only by the Andhra Pradesh government, stands at 2 per cent. This also justifies the concentration of FI accounts in AP.

Table 4.3

Typical Offers of Vendors for FI Projects using Smart Cards

	Initial Cost Per A/C	*1st Year*	*Subsequent Years*
Vendor 1*	200	90	30
Vendor 2*	150	65	65
Vendor 3*	145	65	65
Vendor 4	228	185	65
Vendor 5#	155	20	NA
Vendor 6#	228	NA	NA
Vendor 8#	115	30	30

Note: * These vendors were offering the technology as well as the business correspondent service.
These vendors were offering technology only.

Table 4.4

Back End Costs of the Bank Per No-frills Account Per Year

	XYZ Bank INR Per Account
Training	1.11
Administrative	7.00
Back Office Technology Cost	3.44
Cash Management	1.42
Total Per Account	12.97
Total Per Account for 2 yrs	25.94

Note: In a scale rollout (e.g. AP), this cost is likely to go down by 50 per cent.

The per transaction cost for smart card accounts and plastic card accounts are Rs. 166.15 and Rs. 18.84, respectively. Again, if the same were computed just for live accounts, the cost per transaction are Rs. 262.25 and Rs. 169.60, respectively.

The analysis above is so far based on the technology (smart/plastic) being used to arrive at the costs. There is an upcoming purely mobile based (cardless) model wherein the per account cost comes down to Rs. 30.82. Given these numbers, the cost of including 111.55 million rural households ranges between Rs. 26,319 million for smart card and Rs. 3,438.42 million for cardless (Table 4.5).

Table 4.5

Cost of Financial Inclusion Using Different Technologies (2 Years) Currently Being Paid by the Banks (i.e., Vendor Costs in Table 4.3 + Backend Costs in Table 4.4)

Number of Households to be covered (Mn)		111.55
	Cost Per Account	*INR (Mn)*
Smart Card Based	235.94	26319.11
Plastic Card Based (required as a photo ID)	45.82	5111.67
Purely Mobile Based (data stored on BC's mobile)	30.82	3438.42

All the costs are based on what the banks are actually paying to vendors (BCs). However, by all accounts, these costs are unsustainable in the short to medium term for the BCs. Refer to Table 4.6 detailing the unit cost derived out of the AP case. The gap at the end of two years is Rs. 26.25 per account and the peak deficit happens in the fourth quarter as Rs. 44.29 per account. A two-year view of this is reflected in Table 4.7.

Table 4.7

Actual Cost Equations Using Plastic Cards (2 Yrs)

	Per Account
Plastic Card Based - BC Accounts - Outflows	127.90
Plastic Card Based - BC Accounts - Inflows	101.65
Gap	-26.25

Table 4.8

Breakeven Cost Equations Using Plastic Cards (2 Yrs)

Number of Households to be Covered (Mn)		111.55
	Per Account	*INR (Mn)*
Breakeven Cost Equation Using Plastic Cards (2 yrs)		
Plastic Card Based (Required as a Photo ID) A	45.82	5111.22
Gap Funding Required—Assuming 1.75 Per cent Transaction Fee is being Provided for EBT B	26.25	2928.19
Additional Gap Funding Required In Case No Transaction Fee is being Provided for EBT C	47.2	5265.16
Total B + C	73.45	8193.35
Total A + B + C	119.27	13304.57

Table 4.6

Snapshot of a Typical Financial Inclusion Outlet Financed by a BC (Per Gram Panchayat, Taking Typical Numbers from Andhra Experience)

			Q1	Q2	Q3	Q4	Q5	Q6	Q7	Q8
ROLLOUT										
No. of Customers Who will Open Accounts	1,000		300	250	150	100	50	50	50	50
Active Government Beneficaries* (Incremental)	350		150	100	50	25	25	-	-	-
Government Customers (Cumulative)			150	250	300	325	350	350	350	350
Non-Government Customers (Incremental)	550		150	150	100	75	25	50	50	50
Non-Government Customers (Cumulative)			150	300	400	475	500	550	600	650
All Customers (Cumulative)			300	550	700	800	850	900	950	1,000
Active Non-Government Customers (per cent)			-	-	-	5 per cent	15 per cent	25 per cent	40 per cent	50 per cent
Active Non-Government Customers (Number Billable)			-	-	-	24	75	138	240	325
Benefit Disbursals Per Quarter Per CSP			-	-	240,000	360,000	450,000	500,000	550,000	600,000
OUTFLOWS										
One Time Cost Per Unit			-							
1 Equipment Capex Including GPS and Solar Charger Units	22,500	One time	22,500							
2 Equipment Maintenance							600	600	600	600
3 Recruitment, Interviews, Training, Manuals			2,500							
4 Cost Per Enrollment + Photo-ID Card (Plain Plastic)	20	One time	6,000	5,000	3,000	2,000	1,000	1,000	1,000	1,000
Recurring Costs Per Unit										
1 Fee for Disbursals (0.5 per cent) Paid as Revenue Share to CSP	0.50 Per cent	per txn	-	-	1,200	1,800	2,250	2,500	2,750	3,000
2 Minimum CSP Remuneration	1,000	Per month	3,000	3,000	3,000	3,000	3,000	3,000	3,000	3,000
3 Mobile Data Connectivity	100	Per month	300	300	300	300	300	300	300	300
4 Cost of Consumables	50	Per month	150	150	150	150	150	150	150	150

contd...

contd...

			Q1	Q2	Q3	Q4	Q5	Q6	Q7	Q8
5 Front-end Support Costs (Local Support Unit, Cash Management, District Unit)	1,000	Per month	3,000	2,750	2,500	2,250	2,000	1,750	1,500	1,250
6 Back-end Support Costs (Data Centre, Operations Team, Establishment)	750	Per month	2,250	2,000	1,750	1,500	1,250	1,000	800	650
7 Corporate Office and Management	750	Per month	2,250	2,000	1,750	1,500	1,250	1,000	800	650
Qtr-on-Qtr Outflow Per Unit			41,950	15,200	13,650	12,500	11,800	11,300	10,900	10,600
Cumulative Outflow Per Unit			41,950	57,150	70,800	83,300	95,100	106,400	117,300	127,900
INFLOWS										
Unit Revenues										
1 Opening of Accounts, Delivery of Cards, Initial Active Card Billing	30.00	One time	9,000	7,500	4,500	3,000	1,500	1,500	1,500	1,500
2 Disbursal Fee for Government @ 1.75 per cent	1.75 per cent	Per txn	-	-	4,200	6,300	7,875	8,750	9,625	10,500
3 Technology Fee (Billed on Active non-Govt. Customer Base)	3.60	Per month	-	-	-	257	810	1,485	2,592	3,510
4 BC+BF Activity for Banks (Savings, Withdrawals, Remittances, etc.)			-	-	2,000	2,250	2,500	2,750	3,000	3,250
Qtr-on-Qtr Inflow Per Unit			9,000	7,500	10,700	11,807	12,685	14,485	16,717	18,760
Cumulative Inflow Per Unit			9,000	16,500	27,200	39,007	51,692	66,177	82,894	101,654
							Breakeven			
CASH DEFICIT										
Cashflow Deficit per Unit (Needs a Grant, Soft Loan or Equity Investment)			32,950	40,650	43,600	44,294	43,409	40,224	34,407	26,247
						Peak Deficit				

Notes for present costs incurred by ZMF+ALW:

1 Present Front end costs Rs. 80 lakhs per month for 8200 outlets. Decreases with scale.
2 Present Back end costs Rs. 60 lakhs per month. Per CSP impact will decrease with scale.
3 Present corporate office Rs. 60 lakhs per month. Per CSP impact will decrease with scale.
* NREGA job card holders who enroll for bank account but do not seek work are counted in general non-govt. category.

Breakeven Analysis (for Table 4.6)

1. Each BC outlet requires an initial cash investment of about Rs. 45,000. This is for capex (equipment, initial training) and opex (salaries, consumables, communications, support, back end, management). It is quite clear that banks are not interested in investing this capital. Nearly all banks put the onus of this entire investment squarely on the BC.
2. To the above cash deficit, an additional Rs. 5,000 must be added for the time-gap between billing by BC and payment by bank.
3. Thus, a total cash deficit of about Rs. 50,000 is caused in the first year for each outlet. This deficit will decrease steadily after one year, as revenues build up.
4. With normal projected costs and revenues (through Government disbursals and other basic banking services), a unit can achieve quarter-on-quarter cash breakeven in the fifth quarter. This assumes that larger scale of operations reduces the per unit cost burden of support back-end and management expenses.
5. It will take about three years for a business breakeven (to wipe out accumulated losses).
6. This operating cost of a unit is lower than any other method of providing banking services. Rural bank branches can cost about 50 to 100 times more per year to run.

The country needs about 250,000 such outlets to cover all *gram panchayats* and therefore, effectively serve the entire rural population for basic banking and delivery of government benefits. The technology and deployment model is very scaleable once the investment model is taken care of. Rs. 500 crore (as a 7 year loan or as equity investment) will set up 100,000 dedicated outlets in a matter of 18-24 months, and can transform the face of financial services in rural areas.

The same can be achieved at half the investment (Rs. 250 crore) if the BC can manage to build additional revenue streams which are not strictly part of the banking and financial services domain (such as retail distribution for telcos, insurance companies, FMCG companies, cooperatives, etc). However, this approach may take longer and will bring dependence on many external factors.

The gap of Rs. 26.25 is applicable only in the case of AP where a transaction fee of 2 per cent is being paid. In other cases, the gap widens to Rs. 73.45 per account and full coverage of 111.55 million households would require a gap funding of Rs. 8193.35 million. Where a transaction fee is paid, the gap would only be Rs. 2928.19 million (Table 4.8).

Given this gap, the ways the BC could cover it include the following possibilities:

1. Access to venture funding:

   Since a BC is a not-for-profit company, there are no takers.

2. Access to strategic investors:

   There is a cap of 10 per cent corporate holding in a BC. As a result, few would be attracted as this does not count as strategic investment at all.

3. Fund the viability gap:

   a) Through the FITF Fund.

   b) By making a transaction fee for NREGA and other social benefit payments mandatory.

c) banks could proactively engage the BCs in loan services, including recovery (at say, a recovery fee of 20 per cent for NPAs which are written off in the bank books), insurance, etc. The business case is strengthened only if existing direct accounts (SHG, no-frill, micro-credit, GCC-linked) opened by the bank are handed over to BCs, thereby making the BC an extension service of the bank.

4. The banks foot the entire bill of infrastructure and technology and also pays service charges and transaction fee to the BCs. This can be recouped by the bank in the following ways:

   a) End-user charges, collected on behalf of the bank by the BC.

   b) Allowing banks to charge an interest rate in the band of PLR+5 per cent for loans below Rs. 200,000.

   c) Augmentation of loans and deposits' business volumes.

The issue of covering the viability gap was discussed at length in the research meetings and it was observed that the technology provider and the BC are basically the same organisation, forced to function under two legal entities while for all practical purposes dealing with banks as a single entity. If the BCs are allowed to function as a unified for-profit entity, the problem of attracting funds is addressed to a great extent.

There was a consensus that the viability issue needs to be addressed with a great sense of urgency. Otherwise, with the possible folding up of some of the BCs would create unmanageable bottlenecks in states like Andhra Pradesh, stall financial inclusion initiatives in other states and shake the public confidence in financial inclusion goals.

There is certainly a case for expanding the definition as also exploring all channels such as PRIs, information kiosks, etc., becoming BCs from the point of outreach and not from cross-subsidisation by relying on their existing bouquet of services.

The various positive features of the kiosk-based channel identified during discussions in the context of financial inclusion, were:

- Appropriate linkage between livelihoods and microfinance services.
- Minimises the disbursement, management and monitoring costs by using local human resources and maximises the use of existing infrastructure (i.e. CSCs).

- Enhances livelihood options by establishing kiosks, providing access to financial services and making business information available to the poor.
- Promotes sustainable livelihood systems by building the management capacities of kiosk owners at the grassroots.
- Provides an in-built monitoring mechanism.
- Can be easily replicated.
- Facilitates clients for information and communication.
- Suitable for banks and financial agencies as the risks are shared with kiosk owners, and the repayment rate is high (generally 100 per cent).

There does seem to be a misplaced optimism about specified individual category BCs and NGOs taking financial inclusion to scale. This is not borne out by the experience of the past two years. While SHG-Bank linkages have to encouraged and strengthened in the overall developmental plan, making SHGs into BCs is not recommended. It was felt that SHGs are good as a risk mitigation mechanism and as productive users of credit. If SHGs were to act as BCs, both these advantages are lost.

MFIs have been allowed as BCs, but few have opted for it as the revenue model is not at all attractive. Banks are also wary since they feel MFIs are likely to walk away with their customer base. But the BC model diminishes the argument for regulation to facilitate deposit collection by MFIs, because it will make the service of small deposits, particularly pass book savings accounts, available to low income clients, along with microcredit and other microfinance services. In practice, it will take some time to work out the mode of operations of the BC model because the level of fees and a series of rules governing such operations will need to be determined. More important, with investment and infrastructure costs currently being borne by the BCs, substantially increases operating expenses for NGO-MFIs.

Large development NGOs, while ideally suited to the task, have also shied away because just EBTs does not suit their developmental agenda, credibility issues, payment of deposits and guarantees, etc. An NGO which wanted to make use of the Financial Inclusion Technology Fund (FITF), to facilitate financial inclusion through Village Knowledge Kiosks (Citizen

Centres) faced a problem in the existing policy, in that the proposal has to be submitted to NABARD through a bank and the grant eligible is only 25 per cent and the participating agency should bear 75 per cent. It was suggested that NGO-MFIs should be made as an eligible agency to submit the proposals directly under the FITF, as then it can take up innovative need based projects for financial inclusion. The eligible grant portion should be raised to 75 per cent for big NGOs/MFIs and for small NGOs/MFIs, it should be 90 per cent and the margin from the promoting agency should be brought down so as to ensure that the creativity of an agency should not be limited because of resource constraints. Innovations should be encouraged with lot of in-built flexibilities. Also, banks ask security deposits from BCs and really committed NGOs without adequate financial resources are not able to provide the security deposit to the banks. Hence, the guarantee cover available under the credit guarantee fund trust may be extended to cover BCs also.

The experience of most NGOs using the BC model showed that the commission offered to NGO-MFIs is sometimes inadequate to cover all their costs. Additionally, because banks must update their record with all transactions undertaken by the business correspondent model within 24 hours, many NGO-MFIs face difficulties adhering to this policy. They struggle due to the hard terrain they operate in and low levels of technology penetration at the point of transaction with the client. The proposed MF bill does not allow MFIs to provide savings services. Registered MFIs can offer "thrift" services. Thrift does not include voluntary withdrawable savings as per the proposed bill.

There were also out-of-the-box suggestions as to why should BCs be the only model. The point is that conventional banking has not worked, brick and mortar has not worked, so we need technology, we need BCs and we need BFs. But is it only a question of finding out how to make the BC or BF system work better or is it time to ask a more fundamental question: is this the only way to go, are there other ways and better ways to go? BCs and BFs are only a means. Let us go back once again and revisit the question of ends. What do we mean by financial services? To some, it means giving credit facility to the individual; to some, it means just opening a bank account; to some, it means enabling him to have a savings account; and to others, it could mean just enabling him to make a financial transaction: somebody to pay him or him to pay somebody; any or all of these are part of financial inclusion.

The postal system too has the necessary outreach and presence to implement FI directly. India Post with more than 1,55,000 post offices with 80 per cent of them in rural areas has one of the largest field forces in India with about 3,00,000 *grameen dak-sevaks* and over 2,00,000 postal employees catering mostly to the rural areas of the country. The World Bank's Rural Finance Access Survey (2004) reveals that post office branches in India have the closest proximity to rural clients compared to branches of banks. In Andhra Pradesh, the government has chosen to migrate the disbursements of EBT by post offices to bank affiliated BCs, as the post office system is entirely manual, takes long and cannot provide proper MIS in time. Nationally too, the Department of Posts has chosen to enter in as a BC in a few pilot cases, and not independently as the system automation required is yet to come and revenue is not commensurate with the effort required coupled with their low risk appetite. It should further be noted that for opening a new account, a post office gets Rs. 117 from the government besides whatever else it is getting as a BC. This is not available to a regular BC.

In January 2009, the State Bank of India (SBI) had taken the lead and decided to scale their alliance with India Post by a pan-India rollout of their existing arrangement for providing banking and financial services to the financially excluded population of the country. State Bank of India would develop the financial products and provide training to the postal staff while India Post (which acts as the BC) would source and carry out preliminary processing of applications. The verification, sanctioning and recovery functions would continue to be done by SBI. India Post would service the deposit accounts as a Customer Service Point for transactions (deposits and withdrawals) using handheld Point of Sale devices and receive remuneration (in the form of commission) for all products sourced and services rendered. At present, the alliance covers over 800 post offices and has sourced business of Rs. 25 crore loans, Rs. 8 crore of deposits and over 1,00,000 smart card based 'no-frill' accounts. Moving forward, the alliance plans to include over 80,000 post offices (by March 2012).

Experience with India Post too has been varied. While feedback from Tamil Nadu has been very positive, in one or two other places the complaint was that the post office was just not interested.

The other out-of-the-box suggestion was to allow telcos to directly handle payments, remittances, small savings and other micro-products. Regulatory purposes maybe served by limiting the amounts, number of transactions, etc.

Given its functionality, mobile telephony growth has been extraordinary recently in both rural and urban areas: rural tele-density has increased to 12.72 from 0.4 and urban tele-density 72.47 from 5.8 in past 10 years. India is the fastest growing mobile market in the world and almost 15 million subscribers are being added per month, mostly in rural areas. Such massive growth in numbers is commendable by itself, and if accompanied by the predictable positive economic impact, the results could be unprecedented. Several studies have quantified the role of mobile phones in improving productivity, employment, profits and also enabling social change. The reasons, mobiles have such major impacts, are mainly due to reduction in transaction cost, widening markets and alleviating infrastructure constraints. Each of these positive characteristics of increased connectivity has potential in the financial services sector as well.

Undoubtedly, mobile phones are reaching the customers much more rapidly than envisaged and soon, even the poorest will have a mobile phone in the next 2-3 years. If that be the case, and if you have backend servers at the banks, then one doesn't need any technology other than the mobile phone. The question is, can poorer people who are not necessarily literate use mobile phones? The answer is yes. Already, demonstration systems are available. One answers questions on phone, talks to the bank's computer and identifies oneself uniquely. Voice authentication fortunately is reaching and becoming superior to even the fingerprint. If you have a mobile phone, the CLI of a mobile phone also becomes one authentication point. After that you need basically a PIN. Instead of PIN, voice authentication is far superior and acts as a unique identifier. Once you are able to uniquely identify and are able to talk in your local language with your local dialect to a bank and carry out the transaction, the pace of inclusion will be so much faster.

Another recurring theme in this context of identity, i.e., financial inclusion for whom, who the person is and how to identify that person? There is an initiative which is currently underway in the government for issuing a unique identity to every individual. Everyone will be identified, will have a unique number and there would be a national database with the names, identity numbers and photographs available which could be accessed by authorised people including financial sector institutions, and possibly over the next 3-4 years after that with biometric data also.

In India, where it is expensive and cost ineffective to extend the coverage of the banking channel, branchless payment systems can dramatically reduce the cost of delivering financial services to poor people. Branchless banking can offer basic banking services to customers at a much lower cost than what it would cost to serve people through traditional channels. For the spread of any technology used to increase financial access, it is imperative that the technology is user-friendly and in tune with mass customer needs.

The Institute for Development and Research in Banking Technology (IDRBT), an arm of the RBI, is developing common and interoperable standards for all banks in the country. A draft is expected to be released by July 2009.

To ensure financial inclusion, there are two considerations—open standards and open access—which are very important in terms of defining a standard. Not because these standards are going to impact on what we are doing today, but they are going to impact what we are going to do in the future. They will impact the generations to come in terms of the nominations, in terms of the accounts, in terms of rural population being included as a part of financial systems.

New technologies including mobiles phones, smartcards and fingerprint recognition technology have the potential to give some of the poorest people in the world access to the basic financial services that they have lacked for too long. 'Branchless banking' allows an individual to have a remote bank account that is accessed and managed through their mobile phone or other technologies. This could mean those with no chance of using traditional banks—because they are either too poor or the nearest bank is miles away—will be given the opportunity to save money, gain access to credit and receive money sent from family members in cities.

The key is to ensure that the technology being used at the last mile is accessible, affordable and adaptable.

Over the last few years, regulators have focused on the use of bank agents (or "business correspondents") and more recently, mobile payments as a means to reach the unbanked. Today, India has all the ingredients for making branchless banking work: a government committed to increasing access, a central bank cognisant of the potential and risks posed by branchless banking models, a large, sophisticated banking sector, a dynamic and competitive mobile phone industry, and no lack of cutting edge technology providers.

However, restrictions applicable to the bank agent model have impeded its use. In addition, the potential for payment and mobile banking services to be provided by mobile network operators and other non-banks has not yet been realised due largely to restrictions on non-banks accepting funds from the public and the prohibition on e-money issuance by non-banks.

All this only solves the problem of access to financial services. It does not meet the goal of financial inclusion, and certainly not poverty alleviation.

5 Converting Financial Access to Financial Inclusion

Stakeholder feedback revealed that a huge part of the problem was that end users, clients, target beneficiaries simply did not understand what an account was meant for; they didn't understand what a passbook really means. So when this business facilitator comes to the village, opens an account for them and gives them a passbook, they just don't know what to do next.

Inclusive Economics, Inclusive Governance

There is a need to take a consolidated view of all the learning, fill in the gaps and suggest a common path moving forward. The Skoch model for inclusive growth argues for inclusive economics and inclusive governance as the way forward for inclusive growth. From the financial side, it essentially spans micro-products (e.g. pensions, savings, investments, insurance, credit etc.), technology (e.g. computers, connectivity, mobiles, cards etc.), outreach mechanisms (e.g. BCs/BFs, MFIs, post offices, telecentres, local bodies, NGOs, cooperatives, banks etc.) coupled with a financial literacy umbrella.

From the governance side, it looks at enhancing absorptive capacity, empowerment and economic enablement of SHGs as well as individuals—be it through social spending or any other appropriate development interventions. Role of participatory democracy cannot be undermined in the process.

Mani Shankar Aiyar, then Minister of Panchayati Raj said, "We cannot achieve inclusive growth without inclusive governance and inclusive economics. There is a need to strengthen the Panchayati Raj institutions to ensure development of the poor and underprivileged section of the society."[1]

1. Mani Shankar Aiyar, Minister of Panchayati Raj, Government of India at the Skoch Summit India @ Work, October 2008.

Skoch Model of Inclusive Growth

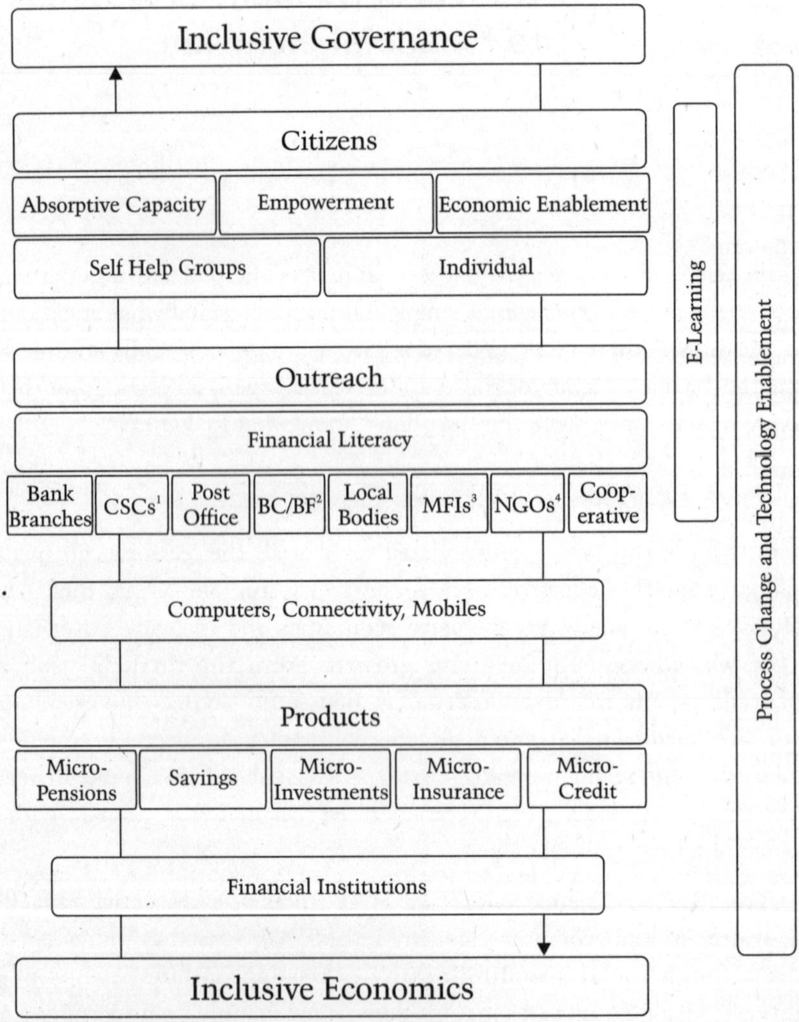

Note: 1. Common Services Centre.
2. Business Correspondent/Business Facilitator.
3. Micro Finance Institutions.
4. Non-Governmental Organisations.

Source: Kochhar, Sameer, R. Chandrashekhar, K.C. Chakrabarty, Deepak B. Phatak (2009). *Financial Inclusion*. New Delhi: Academic Foundation.

Financial inclusion is not a one-off event. In terms of finance provision, it means that hitherto excluded people—either as individuals or as groups—now have access to credit on a regular basis for as long as they continue to abide by the terms of such a credit relationship. For financial inclusion to promote growth, it has to move from "opening an account" in the bank, to regular savings and finally to a relationship which enables the borrower to access loans on a regular basis.

In the hullabaloo about financial inclusion, let us not forget that the rural poor and those on the margin have major problems to achieve food security entirely from an agricultural base. Therefore, for a financial policy to focus only on loans for agriculture and related activities, will not open all the windows that these families require to be included into the financial system. It needs to also focus on livelihood options. Given the seasonal and increasingly uncertain sources of livelihood options that leave gaps in the income/input flow of these families, focusing on 'livelihoods' alone is also not adequate; they also need credit to 'live', to have access to credit for consumption and for urgent needs like illness in order to survive.

Financial inclusion is essential because of its implications for the welfare of citizens, but it needs to be stressed that it has to be an explicit strategy for fostering faster economic growth in a more inclusive fashion. The strategy of financial inclusion has to be placed in the wider context of economic growth and financial deepening.

The landscape of rural India is a very large canvas. There have been an immense number of pilot programmes that have been done across villages. Each of them has achieved success in their own measure. The challenge comes when we have to upscale these projects and make them effective across 600,000 villages.

Financial Literacy

Financial literacy or financial education can broadly be defined as "providing familiarity with and understanding of financial market products, especially rewards and risks, in order to make informed choices. Viewed from this standpoint, financial education primarily relates to personal finance to enable individuals to take effective action to improve overall well-being and avoid distress in matters that are financial."[2]

---

2. Reddy, Y.V. (2006). "The Role of Financial Education: The Indian Case", Address at the International Conference on *Financial Education, OECD and Pension Fund Regulatory and Development Authority*, New Delhi, September 21.

Financial literacy goes beyond the provision of financial information and advice. The focus of any discussion on financial literacy is primarily on the individual, who usually has limited resources and skills to appreciate the complexities of financial dealings with financial intermediaries on a day-to-day basis.

Harvard Professor Shawn Cole and CMF Research Associate Nilesh Fernando recently wrote a very interesting paper[3] that reviews how levels of financial literacy education affect financial behaviour. The paper uses several assessments, both from the developed and developing world, to discuss the consequences of low levels of financial literacy, its effect on savings and investments, and current efforts to improve financial literacy.

According to Cole and Fernando, a significant body of evidence demonstrates a strong link between financial literacy and household well-being. Accordingly, survey findings consistently show that households with low levels of financial literacy borrow at high interest rates, do not tend to plan for retirement, and acquire fewer assets.

Financial literacy plays a significant role in the efficient allocation of household savings and the ability of individuals to meet their financial goals. It also means the ability to seek sound financial advice. In India, the need for financial literacy is even greater considering the low levels of literacy and the large section of the population, which still remains out of the formal financial set-up.

For sustaining financial inclusion, the financial literacy becomes a very critical component. There is a need to simultaneously focus on the financial literacy part besides delivery/access. Our discussants and research findings have revealed that the low level of financial literacy is one of the reasons why the financial inclusion drive has not picked up. While ensuring that the entire unbanked population of India becomes financially literate seems like a formidable task, ensuring that the unbanked population hears about the drive, the benefits of a savings account and how to use one seems much more achievable. Similarly, studies have shown that how accounts opened through the BC model are not being used, after account opening. Certainly, innovative forms of marketing which explain

---

3. *http://www.adb.org/Documents/Periodicals/Microfinance/finance-200803.pdf*

the product in simple terms so that target account holders understand the account and its benefits should go a long way.

In the short term, we may need to reorient our financial literacy material and content to focus on explaining products, especially simple ones, to the people in a manner that they can understand, enabling them to make an informed choice about whether or not to use it. This does not imply that financial literacy isn't important. While small borrowers such as microfinance clients typically use very simple products, there are other low-income groups such as subprime borrowers who become the target clientele for complicated loans which may require a much higher level of sophistication. But, making people financially literate takes time, and by giving people information in a form that they can use, usage patterns may improve.

Credit Counselling Centres: The RBI has asked both the private as well as public sector banks to set up more Financial Literacy and Credit Counselling Centres (FLCC) in every district and has suggested the lead banks to hold a public meeting every quarter in each district to address grievances of the bank customers.[4] These centres should provide both pre- and post-credit counselling—a guidance centre on various development opportunities and support initiatives of the banks and other agencies and credit as a means of a sustainable economic empowerment, credit utilisation and repayment ethics/repayment culture. Post-credit counselling should be on management of finances and debt servicing in times of unexpected losses and natural disasters (like drought, flood, etc.). Lead banks are expected to open a Financial Literacy and Credit Counselling Centre (FLCC) in every district where they have lead responsibility.

RBI's high level committee headed by deputy governor Usha Thorat has made this recommendation in its report based on the feedback that barring a few, most of the operational centres were not performing the intended role and were promoting the bank's products, providing investment advice etc. Also, arm's length distance with the parent bank was not maintained by some centres, which often gave an impression that such centres were an integral part of the bank.

---

4. "Banks Must Promote Financial Literacy: RBI", *The Financial Express*, May 28, 2009.

The counselling centres should have the facility for online submission of applications, which may be forwarded to the branches.

As quality of service is an important aspect, it is desirable to have appropriately benchmarked quality standards for credit counsellors and counselling agencies. Like-wise, it would also be desirable to have a system of accreditation of counsellors. Once setting up of counselling centres gather momentum, they could consider forming an association of credit counsellors.

While the FLCCs would provide financial literacy and credit counselling, the activities of the Rural Development and Self employed Training Institutes (RUDSETI) towards skill development/capacity building could be dovetailed with FLCCs initiatives, for increasing the earnings/debt repaying ability of the distressed borrowers' families.

While credit counselling services may be provided by banks both in rural and urban areas, it is observed that a large segment of the Indian population is resident in rural areas with literacy levels lower than in urban areas. The rural population is also more dependent on the informal sector for its financing needs. It is necessary that a segmented approach, rather than broad-based generalised approach to counselling for all types of borrowers, is adopted. The centres in rural areas could concentrate on financial literacy and counselling for farming communities and those engaged in allied activities. The centres in metro/urban areas could focus on individuals with overdue in credit cards, personal loans, housing loans, etc.

A great deal of emphasis needs to be given by all the institutions to educate the public of the various schemes/facilities. All forms of publicity press conferences, workshops, publications, websites, road shows, mobile units, village fairs, should be actively explored. A suitable budget needs to be provided by all banks for the purpose. In order to go ahead in a planned manner, a committee on financial literacy and counselling may be set up by the Reserve Bank with members from the Reserve Bank, NABARD, IBA, BCSBI, CIBIL, NGOs working in the area and consumer organisations; this will foster greater collaboration in areas relating to consumer education and protection of consumers' interest.

The scheme of FLCCs needs to be linked up with BC/BF model as the mobility and reach of BC/BF up to the doorsteps of poor will be an important factor of success of this scheme. Besides promoting awareness and giving counselling for credit and savings, it would be good to link FLCCs with insurance companies so that the poor can get information and counselling services from a single door.

Mobile Literacy Vans: The vehicles are intended to take the rural and semi-urban branches to village doorsteps and remote areas. Doorstep counselling and guidance is through the educative material and pamphlets create awareness among the remote rural masses about bank schemes and banking facilities.

Utilising NGOs: As recommended by the Working Group on Rehabilitation of Sick SMEs (Chairman: Dr. K.C. Chakrabarty, April 2008), a scheme for utilising specified NGOs for providing the following services to tiny micro enterprises may be launched by the Government:

a. Training in basic accounting principles and credit management.
b. Training on marketing, technology, design development, packaging, quality control etc.
c. Creation and development of institutions of borrowers like cooperatives etc.
d. Participation in exhibitions and marketing fairs.
e. Development of common facilities for a group.
f. Providing financial assistance for infrastructure creation.

School Curriculum: Urgent need is required to dovetail financial literacy into school curricula at all levels. A pilot programme has been launched recently on financial literacy in Karnataka. The programme, launched by RBI in collaboration with the state government, will involve introduction of financial and related material in the curriculum of schools and colleges. Significant steps would also be taken to make financial literacy a part of non-formal education.

Other Initiatives by RBI: The Reserve Bank has undertaken a project titled 'Project Financial Literacy'. The objective of the project is to disseminate information regarding the central bank and general banking concepts to various target groups, such as, school and college going children, women, rural and urban poor, defence personnel and senior citizens. It would be disseminated to the target audience with the help, among others, of banks, local government machinery, NGOs, schools and colleges through presentations, pamphlets, brochures, films, as also through the Reserve Bank's website. The RBI has already created a link on its website for the common person to give him/her the ease of access to financial information in English and Hindi, and 12 Indian regional languages.

Meeting Credit Needs

Small loans at reasonable interest will probably become one of the key drivers. This could even be small consumption loans so the customer does not have to go to the money lenders or even MFI at 24 per cent, if they can get a 12 per cent to 16 per cent loan largely for consumption purposes. It is well known that most of the MFI loans have been, by and large, for consumption purposes. The second thing is of course getting loans for business, trying to do any kind of business and there the whole issue of business viability becomes very important. Is the business viable, are there enough such businesses that even poor people can take it up and become viable? The key thing to recognise is that the banks would be comfortable in giving loans, only if they make money. For that, some understanding of recovery and credit rating will be crucial components.

Insurance for All

India is among the most under-insured countries in the world. The insurance divide only becomes wider as one moves away from the urban areas into the rural hinterland. Here insurance penetration rate is as low as 3 per cent, among the lowest in the world. This is largely because insurance companies have traditionally targeted their products towards a more easily reachable urban audience. All this is set to change. Tremendous competition for a bigger slice of the insurance market and relatively high market saturation in urban areas has led life insurance sector players to start focusing on rural and semi-urban India. Over 700 million people in 600,000 villages constitute the rural population and a huge opportunity for the private life insurance firms.

According to "Selling Life Insurance in Rural India", a report brought out by the international strategy consulting firm, Celent, the country's under-penetrated rural market holds tremendous growth opportunities for life insurance companies. Revenues are expected to grow as much as four times to Rs. 7.8 billion crore by 2015. However, the report very clearly flags a viable and cost-effective distribution channel, innovative products and methods as being the lynchpin of a possible runaway growth curve in rural insurance. Yet another study carried out by UNDP in 2007 across the three states of Tamil Nadu, Orissa and Rajasthan, projected a total market of between Rs. 62 billion crore and Rs. 84 billion in life insurance, health insurance and other needs such as crop and livestock protection for those earning less than Rs. 80 a day.

Products need to be as simple, easily understood and have the ability to provide coverage as near to the point where these people are.

- Introducing a product at a certain defined premium in a number of regions across the country. At the end of a year, stocktaking of the regions is carried out and depending upon the total claims made in every region, the premiums are either reduced if there have been less claims or increased in the case higher claims.
- A number of companies engaged in selling health insurance products have spent time in setting up and providing a network of hospitals before the actual implementation of the scheme.
- For example, there is a universal health insurance policy which is sold for an individual for Rs. 300 for a family for up to Rs. 500-600, for a cashless mediclaim cover of about Rs. 30,000. Taking a 300 plus administrative costs, say Rs. 350 premium from a villager it is not easy. It is difficult for him to afford it. If we could make it into 12 instalments of Rs. 30 each, it is a much easier sell and more people will go for it.

Surveys carried out by insurance companies in rural areas have revealed a number of learnings for the sector players. These include:

- Insurance companies cannot do individual enrolments and have individual members to come into the schemes.
- Awareness of life insurance products, the surveys reveal is very high, since it is seen as a long-term savings plan with tangible and definite benefits at the end of the tenure and is also marketed aggressively.

- The same does not hold true for general insurance products other than for insurance related to tractors, cattle and vehicles. This is also due to the fact that banks which give loans for these insist on insurance policies. Largely general insurance is perceived as an unnecessary expense, with no long-term benefits except in the case of claims and policies for general insurance exhibit a tendency to lapse after initial subscription.

The major stumbling blocks faced by insurance companies are, the information divide, which severely hampers their efforts to attract people to the insurance products on offer; the paying capacity; lack of a cost effective distribution channel and finally, the bottom lines for the companies involved. The biggest stumbling block by far, is the poor understanding of a rural customer. A case in point is the sale of policies to cover livestock. When the companies sell a policy to cover livestock, they want a certificate from a veterinarian even though the nearest one might be miles away. This lack of understanding of ground reality is often the reason for poor penetration of policies.

Insurance companies have now realised that to make inroads into rural areas they will need to depend on aggregators. The role of the aggregator is an important one, since the company needs a point of contact, a person who has already been working with the local populace and has actually established a lot of trust in the communities that he has worked with.

This calls for a change in the mindset which prevails in the insurance industry, specially relating to claims. Traditionally, claims have been the irritant in most policies. In the normal course of events, the claims department does not pass a claim without a survey report and associated bills. This convoluted process has been a sore point with most customers. The answer lies in the marriage of "the right technology with the right mindset". The new *mantra* for insurance companies today is that if the product on offer is simple, the claims too should be simple.

However, selling insurance in the rural areas through agencies by paying them a 15 per cent incentive, is neither remunerative either for the insurance company or for the insurance agents. It is important to have a cost effective distribution channel to be able to distribute small ticket products. To increase their distribution in the rural areas, some of the other facilitators used by the insurance companies today include, non-government organisations (NGOs) and self help groups (SHGs). Some companies like The Oriental Insurance Company Limited are looking at tapping into the wide network of post offices and postmen across the country to help in the collection of premiums. Despite roping these other facilitators, the insurance companies are finding the going tough and are unable to reach a point where the schemes being promoted become viable. Most insurance companies are coming around to the view that insurance will need to ride on some of the existing policies and financial products. Anyone who takes a bank loan should automatically be insured and this process could be extended to anyone who recharges his mobile card, or even purchases a bus ticket. These add-ons are important to jumpstart the spread of insurance policies.

This is where the role of Information Communication Technologies (ICT) comes to the fore. The need of the day is to devise schemes which will ride on multiple activities such as banking, life insurance and general insurance. There are instances where various organisations are found to be engaged in collection of premiums. They use the General Packet Radio Service (GPRS), a packet oriented mobile data service available to users of Global System for Mobile Communications (GSM) mobile phones in large parts of the remote areas of their operations for their transactions.

Another innovative channel could be the 100,000 Centralised Service Centres (CSCs) for delivering e-governance to 600,000 villages across the country. The Life Insurance Corporation of India (LIC) is already working with a franchising agency which delivers the e-services through CSCs in Kerala. All insurance companies and banks can piggy bank on these, since the CSCs are well distributed geographically and will be connected on a high bandwidth.

Catering to MSMEs

Formal mechanisms to provide financial support to the micro and small industrial sectors are quite limited to agriculture and manufacturing activities. These traditional sectors offer almost no possibility for generating surplus, savings for investments to improve productivity for better income opportunities. Banks have to leverage the opportunities available for micro enterprises in trade and services sectors. Technology centric delivery models will alone be able to cater to the financial needs of the people in rural areas in view of the prohibitive cost involved.

North-east Region

In context of financial inclusion, north-east is becoming key focus areas for almost all institutions such as RBI, NABARD, banks, MFIs, development finance institutions, multilateral organisations and other facilitating actors. However, they often remain unaware about each other's agenda and programmes. This limits the progress of financial inclusion in NER, therefore the inclusion process could not be fast tracked. This requires for more sharing of knowledge, collaborations between different players and convergences of programmes having financial inclusion as a main agenda or at least an important component within a programme.

Some suggestions for achieving financial inclusion in NER are:

- Using BC/BF model extensively along with wireless communication technology to bring down the transaction cost.
- Building capacities of Primary Agriculture Cooperative Societies (PACS) and ensuring their proactive role in financial inclusion.
- Opening special bank branches for SHG financing on the lines of Oriental Bank of Commerce in Uttarakhand.
- Engaging traditional financial institutions in the process of service delivery and enhancing bulk financing to the MFIs for initial take off and on lending.
- Linking microfinance with livelihood sub-sectors (identification and promotion of region specific products) through linkages with suitable partners.
- Innovative linkages of commercial banks with post offices (under BC/BF model).
- Using social capital existing in the form of Village Development Committees.
- Developing pilots on new products and services.

As SEBI chairman, C B Bhave said, "The first step is to include the people living in remote areas in power-sharing. Choice should be theirs."[5]

5. Bhave, C.B. (2008). *Keynote Address at SKOCH Summit 2008*. Mumbai, June 10-11.

FI in Urban Areas

The urban areas are largely outside the Lead Bank Scheme. There is a need for public policy intervention for improvement of financial services in urban areas. However, the concept of tackling financial inclusion in these areas is different. In urban areas, like in Mumbai, there are migrant labourers. These migrant labourers lack the knowledge of banking facilities. What they are looking for besides opening up an account is the facility of remittance. They either make use of these informal methods of remittance or carry cash themselves when they go home. Now that core banking solutions have come, anywhere, anytime banking is possible, there is a need to spread this message especially in the urban metropolitan areas.

If we have to sustain the high rate of growth achieved in recent years and in fact accelerate the growth rate to higher levels, and translate that growth into broad-based poverty reduction, we must address some important challenges. The six challenges on the way forward to accelerating growth and poverty reduction are: stepping up agriculture growth, infrastructure development, fiscal consolidation, enhancing the quality and reach of primary education and basic health, managing globalisation and good governance. Identifying these challenges and drawing up plans to address them is the relatively easy part. What is infinitely more difficult is the translation of those policies into action.[6]

Today, we are at a point that we need to revisit the aims of financial inclusion. It should ensure that actually there is lesser financial disparity and more people in the rural and semi-urban area are able to enjoy the fruits of growth. They, in turn, should be able to provide additional demand because that will definitely expand the market. It will actually ensure the aims of equity in as much that financial inclusion will see that the benefits of growth reach a larger number of people, adding to the strength of the country both economically and in terms of a social fabric. This is also what inclusive development is about.

6. Rangarajan, C. (2009). "Reduce Economic Disparities, Improve Social Indicators", *Inclusion*, April-June, pp.36-39.

6 Summary of Stakeholder Discussions

Business, regulatory and technology issues in the process of financial inclusion were discussed in the focus group discussions, research meetings and a national consultation, which were attended by senior level management of various stakeholders such as banks, financial institutions, industry, technology providers, regulatory bodies, academia and research institutions along with national level BCs and BFs. The discussions have been summarised below as per the research questions. In addition, comments emanating from one-on-one interviews and the e-discussion on the UN Solution Exchange have also been incorporated in the relevant topics. The points below reflect views from across the spectrum, and may even be contradictory. These should not be read as recommendations, which are presented in the next chapter, but as a mirror of current opinions on issues relating to financial inclusion.

Business Scan

How to Make Banking Correspondents (BCs) Viable?

The consensus was that BCs are unviable as of today.

- The business case cannot be in isolation; it should include the bank, the service providers, the business correspondents (BCs) and the end-users.
- We have got a robust financial system in our country. So, banks can take the risk for a certain period of time. For example, this will not be viewed as a business case for the bank, say, for the next five years. After five years, it may break even and thereafter, the banks can earn profits out of this activity. But the technology provider, the BC or the end-use customer may not have the same time periods.

A BC Account from the North-East

I would like to take a specific example of what we are facing today in the North-east. We were asked a few days ago to provide a solution in Jaintia Hills in Meghalaya, a place with lot of open cast coal mines. NREGS is active there. However, according to the Collector and NABARD officials there, it takes about 2-5 months for a person who has done any work to receive his money. This is an area which is completely unmotorable and only a strong four-wheel drive can navigate some of the parts. In the other areas one has to trek. There is no bank for some 70 km from many of these habitations—and this seems more like 500 km in this kind of terrain. At times, it is impossible to move cash, even if you have the money over such distances and banks are willing to give you cash for much more extended period than otherwise they are willing to do, but it is physically impossible. In the rainy season, there is no way that this movement can happen at all. There is no electricity, 80 per cent of the villages don't have electricity. Even if they have connections, it is not available most of the time.

But despite all this, there is mobile connectivity there. There is mobile connectivity from Airtel and BSNL, and mobiles are common. People use solar power extensively to charge their mobiles. Data connectivity is good as both BSNL and Airtel have available GPRS in these locations. Bandwidth is low but it is available. So we were asked to provide a solution here where people can open biometric accounts so that they can be paid in time. Our biggest challenge is cash. We can provide technology but how do we get cash there. Therefore, the only real solution is barter using cashless mode of transaction through the mobile. It is like using your debit or credit card. This can happen offline but it can also happen online. Both modes are possible—that you can provide people a smart card which is also a SIM card and it can be automatically updated online when it is put inside a phone. Outside the phone, it can be used as a regular smart card.

So we are proposing this to NABARD. We have not yet implemented this. These are still early days, where we are trying to figure out exactly what solution to adopt and this is really the kind of place which desperately needs financial inclusion and the services of the correspondents. Some cash services would still be required. The NREGS wages can be directly credited but people will still need to use some cash. Small merchants will need to accept this cashless value but sometimes they will need some cash. For that, a BC would be required. We are still not clear about which banks we will work with as the nearest branch is likely to be 80-90 km away. Branches which are a little bit closer are the Meghalaya Rural Bank and Apex Co-Operative Bank which as everybody would understand are technologically not there at all and they have not participated in this exercise. The other two banks are State Bank of India and United Bank. State Bank is a little bit further, United Bank is a little bit closer. United Bank is more than willing to be a part of it but we are still deciding our strategy.

- One may want to consider some mandatory training for the BCs or whichever channel of distribution, so that they are able to explain all these products in a standardised format.
- Scaling can be actually done in two different ways. One, if the Government decides that it will subsidise or second, if it makes business sense.
- Are banks viable today doing financial inclusion? The answer is no. All the stakeholders, the banks, technology providers, BCs, even the end-users, are all unviable.
- It cannot be viable at this stage. If one asks this question now, it is a disincentive for the entire take-off.
- There could be a possibility to make it viable if the approach taken is little different.
- The objective of financial inclusion is to make available all financial services at affordable cost at their place, but it is not a charity.
- If RBI is really interested in promoting financial inclusion, the state governments should be forced to bear the cost substantially.
- In any business, if it is a viable business, the question is not what it is losing today but what it can make tomorrow because every business starts with losing.

Should Financial Inclusion be Not-for-Profit?

There was consensus that it should be for profit.

- A Section 25 company cannot be for profit. Profit means dividend. Section 25 company cannot declare a dividend. It has no recourse to equity.
- Should the investor get returns? Anything that does not give you some returns cannot be scalable.
- To make it sustainable, it has to be profitable.
- For banks, it has to be viable; whereas for the Government it may not need to be profitable.
- Everyone knows that the Section 25 company is being created and in the back-end, it is the technology service provider who is doing it.

- What is the purpose of putting this Section 25 restriction? Are they more secure or are stable?
- This 'not-for-profit' conditionality is absolutely absurd. Today, one may have a huge infrastructure which one can make use of, whereby the whole life of the financial inclusion can become easier.
- If RBI has some problems/issues that profitable companies will squeeze the public and create a problem for financial inclusion, then the minimum they can do is to remove the restriction of 10 per cent cap on corporate holding.
- BC, *per se*, at least in one's understanding is a meaningless entity which is being created. In the process whatever little margin is available gets further divided creating an inefficient system. It makes it more non-viable than actually making it viable.
- Viability for this particular purpose will have four dimensions. One is that the intervention should be viable for the person who is making the intervention. For example, in this case the banks. Second, it should be viable for the service providers, the people who are assisting to reach that last mile customer. Third, the BC, BF or the technological solution providers and most important is that it must be a viable activity for the end user. The end user is the customer. If one makes the things so loaded and make the things so complex, it will not work. So, viability for the intervention maker, for the service provider, for the end users, the rural customers and viability for the society as a whole.
- BCs for bankers are third parties and they are the face of the bank in rural areas where they are working on behalf of the bank. The bankers are exposed to great risk, including reputation, legal risk and so many other risks. So, there should be a system for rating the BCs and also for training them.
- All these issues arise because the BC and the technology vendor is the same. Ideally the bank should be there, BC should be there. Somebody else should provide the technology.
- If it is for profit, then they can get venture funding, they can get equity investments, so on and so forth. The minute one says that it is a Section 25 company, it does not make profit and does not give

dividend, one does not have access to equity. All these things create restrictions and one does not have recourse to money.

Should Interest Rates be Liberalised?

- Everywhere in the world, wherever microfinance has succeeded, the interest rates are far higher, although they are much lower than the rates that moneylenders charge.
- We are justifying a higher rate of interest for MFIs, taking the argument that the alternative source of borrowing i.e., moneylender, is still higher. Instead, we have to think in those terms where the borrower is viable and at the same time the provider/lender is also viable. Otherwise, the higher rates of interest are not going to sustain in a very long-term.
- For short-term loans, a higher interest rate is viable. For any sustained long-term borrowing, it is not viable.
- Currently, because of the interest rate cap, it is not possible for banks to lend through BCs.

Who Should Pay for the Card?

- Every poor fellow has a mobile but when it comes to the card, we say "How can the poor fellow pay the card cost?" The cost of a card is Rs. 10 or Rs. 50 and the customer cannot bear it but, the mobile costs Rs. 1,000-2,000 and he is able to buy it.
- At present, the banks are bearing the card cost. The customer is not being charged anything.
- Karnataka government is giving Rs. 25 as subsidy for each card. Andhra Pradesh government is also giving some commission.
- The entire cost including the technology cost plus the BC cost is the bankers' cost for the IT-enabled financial inclusion. Technology component comprises the card cost, the CSPs' rental, the wear and tear of those equipments, the data flow and using that, technology platform of the service provider. These costs are technological costs.

Should an End-Customer Charge be Levied?

- The answer to that is, the end user will not pay you if you don't deliver value.

- The RBI specifically says the customer should not be charged. The bank should bear the charge.

Should a Fee for Handling the Banking Transaction be Provided in Social Spending Projects?

- Banks are commercial entities; they have to make some money in the process of handling such payments. What is being talked about here are very small amounts that just get into the bank and go out of the bank. Somebody working under NREGA is not going to have a substantial savings account. He is going to be using quite a bit of that money to consume for immediate needs. We found that only in Andhra Pradesh, the state government had been proactive and had provided for 2 per cent transaction fee to be given to the banks for handling the NREGS payments. In other states, this was not the case.
- The RBI Deputy Governor has written to every Chief Secretary of the state governments that if they consider the 2 per cent commission, they will be paid Rs. 50 per card. But with this condition, so many state governments are not agreeing to it.

Who Foots the Bill for Cash Management?

- The bank is incurring a huge cost. It has to be looked as a business case but it may take some time. Everybody is convinced on this point.

Financial Literacy—Responsibility? Cost?

- There is a difference between financial literacy and financial awareness. Financial literacy is very long-term goal and it may take a very long time to make one billion people in this country financially literate, but it is certainly possible for banks and their BCs, maybe with the *gram panchayats* as well, to organise some sort of training workshop or just introduce the BCs in the village and say, "This person is our agent and is going to help us." Then, it is a valuable proposition even for banks, since there is a lot of reputational risk that is dependent between the BC and the bank relationship.

- A huge part of the problem is that the end users did not understand what an account was meant for. A business facilitator comes to the village, opens an account for them, gives them a passbook but they don't know what that passbook means.
- There is a need for the umbrella of financial literacy because, one may have all the products, but the poor villager does not know them and what can be done with them. In rural India, death means the end, there is no economic future. So, who will teach them what the concept of insurance is? When a cow dies someone is willing to pay, when a house is destroyed in an earthquake someone is willing to pay. They cannot comprehend these things.
- To have a business case in the first place, BCs have to have large manpower, acquiring that manpower is a cost to them, and then training that manpower to do the BC job is again a cost to them. If the manpower is not properly trained, they do not know what they have to do in the village. They are simply told that they have been recruited, they take the account opening form, go to a village, fill that account opening form, they may or may not be in a position to digitise that data. If they are in a position to digitise, they have been told that you digitise and send it to your server and that is all. But that is not the only job a BC agent has to do in a village. It is much larger than this. When a person is visiting a village for financial inclusion as a BC on behalf of a particular organisation, he has to first make the people or the end user understand what the purpose of his visit is and that requires proper training.
- BC will play a very important role in financial literacy. The primary role that they will play is in educating the people on how it can really benefit them.
- If we want no-frills accounts to be used, we need to make the connection between banks and BCs much more productive and we need to make people more aware of the kinds of products that they can use. For that, there is a need for an awareness campaign.
- Where is the need to have separate infrastructure for capacity building and for providing educational and consultancy services? One can have a single institution for the purpose in rural areas

and leverage this for both the purposes. RUDSETIs or FLCCs can be used for both the purposes. They have similar kinds of administrative set-up for both the institutions, only thing is that the state government is participating in RUDSETIs and they are not participating in FLCCs. RBI has got a full set of guidelines for FLCCs but the ultimate purpose is the same for both the institutions, that you want to build the capacity and you want to provide the consultancy services ultimately for financial inclusion so that people can have the knowledge of how to manage their money, how to manage their debts, how to manage their other economic affairs.

- Another view is that, the objective for setting up RUDSETI is totally different; the objective of establishing FLCC is totally different. One cannot combine both.

Product Gaps—Micro-insurance, etc.?

- Too much of our focus has been on PoS, on card and other things and not really on what does banking give you. Small deposits, insurance products, other investment products and far more important, small loans. These are the kind of things with which one needs to go with.
- It is assumed that poor have no need to save. Fact is, they have a more pronounced need to save than all of us.
- Can there be a very low risk kind of a product that the poor could also invest in and get, may be, a better return than savings bank account would possibly offer?
- There is a thinking that, at least 80-90 per cent accounts must have transactions so that we can treat them as live accounts. When these accounts have transactions, one can create a transaction history and based on that, one can take credit decisions.
- One needs to really understand the whole gamut of activities that can be done as a part of financial inclusion and not be restricted to only one activity or one product.
- The banks are also focused on only opening of accounts. There are so many banking products that can be embedded in the process.

Even in terms of RoI, whether from the bank's point of view or any other perspective, one has to focus on the whole activity *per se*.

- To design products, whether savings or investment, one will first have to know the cash flow of that particular area, the activity that is being pursued in that area, so household surveys is the starting point. The working group which was appointed for achieving cent per cent financial inclusion in Goa by RBI has also insisted on quality of financial inclusion, not just on quantitative aspects, targets and all that.
- Microfinance has been successful because they have identified what is the major need of the people. The major need is credit, not savings. If any MFI goes to a village and say "we would like to open savings accounts", the public will not come. There is a need to identify the package that would be offered in financial inclusion and selected on a priority basis. Then other products like insurance, pension, savings can come one by one.
- Any product must first make sense from a customer point of view. The reason why MFIs succeeded is that it gave small loans. Small loans for consumption at reasonable interest will probably become one of the key drivers. Then, the customer does not have to go to the moneylender or even MFI at 24 per cent interest if they can get a 12-16 per cent loan largely for consumption purposes because most of the MFI loans have been, by and large, for consumption purposes.
- Micro mutual funds can also be explored. One example is SBI Mutual Fund at Rs. 100 per month for poor people in rural/semi-urban areas. Here also there is a regulatory problem as PAN number is required.

Possible Additional Revenue Areas for BCs?

- Many BCs are already micro-insurance agents. They are earning a lot of revenue by way of commission.
- There is a need to have certain kind of tie-ups either with the Government for NREGS and social security payments or with Mother Dairy for milk payments or with FCI for food procurement

payment or with some other agency for some other kind of payments so that the transactions in these accounts can be ensured.

- Whatever liberalisation has been done is fine but BC and BF can become the face of the bank in rural areas.
- Till the time a common platform for multiple uses is put in place, nobody will become viable. Even in the case of Common Services Centres (CSCs), viability is under question because they have to be put to multiple uses first.
- Earlier it was being said that a BC's main job is going to be a BC plus he can do photocopying, plus he can do photographs. Today the saying is that the guy who is doing photocopying, who is doing photographs, should be a BC.

Regulatory Issues

Should the Definition of BCs be Enlarged? E.g. Post Offices, CSCs, SHGs, PRIs etc.

Overall view was that the definition of BCs should be enlarged.

- In the BC space, the biggest challenge today is their restricted number. There are a countable few who are eligible to be the BCs, who really have the capabilities and who have proved that they can work on a larger spectrum.
- The post office and the Panchayati Raj Institutions can be used. There cannot be any restriction on who should be what. Without exploring the various approaches which are available for this, no beginning can be made in financial inclusion.
- RRBs and their branches and post office branches are the direct connection to the end user. They should be used for human interaction-related banking activities and completely disregard them for technology-related issues. Transactions may be done straight between the end user and the backend central systems. That is precisely where the mobile comes in as the most important component in the whole thing. Why does one need RRBs to be even aware of what technology is being used for doing transactions? Instead they should do all the support work that is required, for

example, KYC norm, any paper work, any recording of photograph, any forwarding of information, etc. The minimal technology that they require can be provided by a PC based interface. But as long as transactions are concerned, they happen even on behalf of rural banks from the backend exchanges which could be set in the controlling banks of these RRBs.

- CSC should be approved as one of the eligible entities to become the BC of banks so that one more function can be added to their whole lot of activities. They are already in the perfect position.
- Banks find it extremely difficult to pilot any proposal within the bank because a bank has to sign an agreement only with a legal entity. It cannot sign an agreement with a loose confederation which is not recognised.
- The SHG is a consumer of credit. If they become BCs, then the disburser and consumer of the credit and the person responsible for recovery becomes the same.
- SHGs may be an important component of the entire system but what is being debated is their role as BCs and it appears that their role as BC is a limited one and may not even be viable. They may not be able to discharge that duty.
- Panchayati Raj Institutions qualify on all the counts, they have an office, they are savvy and they can handle money.
- Any number of new players can be added. There is no dearth of varieties of BCs which can be appointed or used. Ultimately, the basic thing is that they are playing with the public money because when the customer pays Rs. 100 to a BC, he is not paying the BC; he is paying the bank. Once he gives Rs. 100 to the BC, he thinks his account should be credited. That's all he wants.
- Well established *kirana* shops with registered number can be considered in order to enlarge the scope and outreach of financial inclusion.
- There is a need to look at various types of BCs in different geographies across India. One model will not succeed.
- Village cooperative credit societies can act as a correspondent for commercial banks. Studies should look at ways to provide the appropriate linkages and revive these societies.

Should the 30 km Norm be Changed?

After considerable discussion, the consensus was that the 30 km distance norm was adequate.

- Regulator has come out with the appointment of BCs and BFs to facilitate the whole process. This is an emerging area and they are also in the learning phase. Earlier, they fixed a limit of 15 km for BC operations from the base branch, now they have relaxed it up to 30 km. Subsequently, further relaxations may also come. They have also further simplified the KYC norms. So, all these things are gradually coming and one has to go along with this at least for five years.
- The distance is important as the entire burden of getting the cash is on the BC; the bank does not help. The BC has to travel to the bank, get the cash and bring it. There is a cost involved in that also.
- The point to be addressed is that the entire norm got changed from 15 to 30 km because people said that outreach is not happening. Somewhere one suspects that the bankers' interest was kept in mind when they changed it from 15 to 30 because they said now the banks' outreach will improve. But, it is not a necessity that the bank's infrastructure will reach those 30 km.
- This 30 km will not work in the north-east and other interior areas.
- There should be no restriction at all. Where is the need to restrict to any radius area?
- Increasing the limit serves no purpose as cash management will only become more difficult.

Should NBFCs, etc., be Allowed as BCs?

The general view was that most NBFCs would not be interested in becoming BCs.

- There is a need to think about whether or not there is a business case for NBFCs, which are the largest providers of microfinance in the country right now, to become BCs.
- None other than Dr. Rangarajan had suggested that microfinance NBFCs should be made BCs for the limited purpose of garnering

deposits and remittances for banks. One has been persistently following it up, but it is unlikely to happen.

- If NBFCs become BCs, there will be a clash of interest. Experience in some states with an NBFC has been discouraging. They came out, did some BC work, but mainly they propagated their own products and went away.
- The recommendation of Rangarajan Committee has not been accepted by the government.
- The popular thinking is that most NBFCs and MFIs don't want to be BCs.
- The first best option would always be to allow NBFC, MFIs to accept savings after making sure that there are enough prudential guidelines and things like that. The second best option is to allow them to act as BCs who then collect deposits, except that most NBFC, MFIs would not be interested.
- The fact is that NBFCs are not allowed to mobilise savings. But why not use these entities that are anyway in touch with the customers for their lending purposes.
- Somewhere for an NBFC, the lines will become blurred. Then the next thing the NBFC is going to say is, "Why can't I actually run like a bank?"
- When MFIs can become microfinance NBFCs, why can't NBFCs become banks? There should be more microfinance banks in India. But, they should lend at the same rate that banks are lending to the poor.
- NBFCs engaged in microfinance activities should be recognised as a separate institution.
- The reason why NBFCs are not allowed to take savings deposits from people or open savings accounts is that they are in lending business. They are risking their own money in lending to somebody in the hope of getting better returns because the interest rates are high. But when they are taking deposits, it is the customer who is risking money with them and that is the fundamental issue. That is why there is a whole category of NBFCs which are non-deposit

taking NBFCs. They are not allowed to play with the customers' money.

- Ultimately if the poor has to get the services, the entire six lakh villages have to be covered at the reduced cost and the banks alone cannot do so. It should be through the BC mechanism only. All MFIs, NGOs, NBFCs should be encouraged to become BCs. If they do things differently, there should be sufficient disincentive for doing so.
- The popular perception is that microfinance is all about livelihood generation whereas financial inclusion is about the very basic fundamental need to connect a person to the financial institution. So livelihood generation is actually a step further.

Are the Mobile Payment Guidelines Adequate or Restrictive?

- There is one part of the guidelines which may be a little confusing and become a reason for banks not to adopt it in a big way. This is the provision which says that, "the banks must role out these services with multiple operators". It should be mobile operator agnostic as this implies that any technology that is proposed must work right away and be accepted by all the operators.
- It says the telcos are not allowed any store value kind of option. Only banks can go ahead with those store value card or the prepaid kind of an option. But one fine day, it has to come that telcos should be allowed to do various other services apart from prepaid product top up. From that point of view, it is restrictive.
- The Stored Value Card (SVC) is, in fact, more required for the rural environment because in an urban environment, you have everything starting from e-banking to ATM banking and there are various means of making payments and receiving payments. SVC facilities are actually required more in rural India.
- Both the mobile payment guidelines and the prepaid guidelines have to be read together.

Are KYC Norms Adequate or Restrictive?

- What can be simpler than self-attestation?

- In case of NREGS, the government has already done the KYC of these persons and issued them job cards. Now the government says that these people have to be paid through biometric-based accounts. That account may not be in the post office, that account may be in another bank and the bank's process is that no account can be opened unless the customer signs an application form and his photograph is available with the bank. What is suggested is a simpler process which removes one step altogether. Instead of going to the person two times, one goes to the person once or rather the person comes once when he comes to get his money. The government has, for example, enrolled 100 persons in a village for NREGS wages, they have given them job cards and 20 of those people have worked in a particular work cycle. Currently, accounts are opened for all 100 people, which means forms are taken, those forms are filled, signed, their photos are taken and their finger prints are taken. The form is sent to the branch, the data is sent to the central system of the bank and account is opened and a card is made. Then one goes to the village again to give the card to that person. When the wages get credited, the person has to again come forward. So, there are actually three steps where the person needs to get involved. Therefore, the suggestion is to simplify this on the basis of the data that is given by the government. Let the bank be allowed to open provisional accounts. These are not real usable accounts as yet. By this, nobody is flouting any norms here, but it allows opening of provisional accounts for all the 100 people in the bank system right away. The data that the government provides is adequate to open core banking accounts. The SBI core banking system requires nine fields and all these nine fields are actually provided by the government. These are all text based fields and one does not require a photo. So, the person will come only when he has got to collect his money. But, the banks are simply not willing to even consider a change in process.
- Telcos also do KYC while taking customers on board. If this KYC can be considered for financial inclusion this will be a great step towards financial inclusion.
- The RBI's stand on KYC for financial inclusion is much more relaxed than the TRAI's stand on KYC. TRAI requires proper identification,

proof of address, etc. What this will lead to eventually is a situation where a man need not have any other document for the fact that he has a mobile phone in his hand. It will work wonders, with 40 per cent tele-density in this country, if a person has to just go with his phone bill only to open his bank account and the banker accepts that.

Should BCs be Allowed to Work With Multiple Banks, Insurance Companies etc.?

- There should be coordinated effort on financial inclusion for a village or a set of people. The BC who understands that particular village should bring in all the products (no-frill, medical insurance, investment products, etc.) in a structured manner.
- There does not seem to be any restriction that BCs have to work with one bank. A BC can operate for various banks provided there is specific arrangement of functioning.
- If it is in pilot, the regulation should be flexible. It should be given to the bankers, they can be flexible and they can do it their way. When the pilot stage is completed, then all models can be put together and then scaling up will be according to the bank policy.
- In a village normally there is a sponsor bank and accounts are opened in the village only for that sponsor bank but transactions are offered to all member banks. The system works with 22 banks whereby transactions are offered in the village to all the 22 banks but the people open accounts only for one sponsor bank.
- The BC can be used to sell insurance products and also service them. That would require some change in the guidelines because for the service of insurance products you need certain minimum level of literacy and education. IRDA has to understand those limitations also.
- There seems to be lack of interest or lack of focus by the government towards insurance as a financial inclusion tool.

Are There Any Regulatory Hurdles in Combo-Insurance (Life and Non-life) Products?

- LIC is coming out with a Combo Micro Insurance product (life plus cattle insurance and livestock, etc). It will be the first of its kind in the country. Prior to that will be a term assurance product which is right now with IRDA in which the company will not only give term assurance, i.e., one gets an amount immediately on death and if he survives the period, the company refunds the premia, which is a unique thing. So, even if he lives, he gets back his money and if, God forbid, the policy owner dies then he gets the entire amount with in-built accident benefit, etc. That product will be woven into the combo product. But, the regulation insists that a life insurer can tie-up with only one general insurer for a combo product. The general non-life insurance has varying strengths in different parts of the country. They are stronger in some areas, weaker in other areas. So, there is a need for flexibility and freedom that life insurers can tie up with any general insurer for different regions.

- RRBs can become micro insurance agents. There was a Govardhan Committee which had recommended it and people were awaiting the outcome of that. But in the new micro insurance regulation, there is no mention that RRBs can do so.
- Technology is going to be the only saviour for micro insurance. Unless it is total technology driven business, one cannot even break even, forget about becoming profitable. Viability itself will be an issue. So this year LIC is planning to give handheld devices to all the agents.
- Micro insurance regulation does not allow CSCs to be agents. In LIC, the CSC network appoints VLEs (Village Level Entrepreneurs). Those people are trained and while they are doing other work, they also canvass for LIC business.
- Since a CSC covers both these spaces—e-Governance space as well as financial sector—the challenge is that all the CSCs are losing money. None of them are making money.
- The regulatory issue is whether the BC can sell micro insurance products of different insurance companies.
- The rule, that one cannot sell products of different companies, should be waived especially in the case of micro insurance, given the peculiarity of rural infrastructure and the network.
- In the rural insurance sector, the primary problem is availability of products. There is no flexible product available to suit the needs of

the rural customers and is still being developed. The other problem is lack of distribution channels. As a result of the high distribution cost, the rural sector does not become a priority sector for insurance companies. Then, insurance is a promise of providing a service. The servicing cost of insurance products is also very high.

- If banks want to sell insurance, they can earn revenues and insurance companies also get a distribution channel.

Technology Scan

Is Adequate Technology Available?

- Technology fortunately is moving in a direction where the cost will really come down. Everybody wants to reduce the cost of transactions.
- Poorer people who are not necessarily even literate can use a mobile phone. There are already demonstration systems available and in less than a year's time, one will see enough of such systems coming up. This will involve talking on phone, answering questions on phone, talking to the bank's computer one will be able to first identify yourself uniquely. Voice authentication fortunately is reaching and becoming superior to even the fingerprint. If one has a mobile phone, the CLI of a mobile phone becomes one authentication point. After that one basically needs a PIN. Instead of PIN, voice authentication is far superior and uniquely identifies and works out better. Once somebody is able to uniquely identify himself, one is able to talk in local language to a bank and carry out the transaction. In six months to a year, such technologies will become available and will help in scaling.
- The key thing is that should it be totally in local language, with the local dialect, with voice authentication and using simplest mobile phone for calling.
- Voice will end up replacing most platforms.
- It is obvious that the conventional banking system cannot deliver the kind of financial inclusion that is sought for the simple reason that given the economic level of people in the villages and given the density of the population, the conventional brick and mortar

structure of the banking system obviously cannot cover all the people. The banking sector and the RBI have recognised this and come up with innovations like BCs and BFs. There has to be an intelligent combination of all of these things with technology.

- Technology is going to be a huge driver and already there are different ways in which mobile technology has been used to deliver certain kinds of services.
- There are problems because the telcos and service providers are obviously driven by profitability and there are issues of profitability when you go down there. So, how can one make it worthwhile? Is there a way to ensure that it is viable for these companies to really provide mobile services in the rural areas? One approach has been to set up a Universal Service Obligation Fund, under which government requires these companies to go into the rural areas and required financial support is provided to ensure that the business case is viable.
- One has realised over a period of time that technology does not sell by itself unless it is simplified to a point that a common man can understand it, and use it and make it a daily part of his life. That is what adds value. Telcos have shown how it can be done. Even in terms of offering, the product is broken down to such a level that with just Rs. 5, one can actually go and buy talk time. They have simplified the product so that it can be consumed by various people in various modes depending on their capabilities.

Common Platform/Interoperability Issues?

- Every state government should come out with an IT backbone or IT technological platform and the same platform can be used for CSC project, by the banks for financial inclusion, by insurance companies for RSBY and all other things. Otherwise, it will not be utilised to its optimum level.
- Each person seems to be running with his own technology and there isn't a single platform that can go ahead and aggregate or *per se* give an organic platform to all these technologies to be able to interoperate one with the other.

- Today, Suvidha is becoming an interoperability platform between the CSCs. Currently it is the common platform for about 50,000 CSCs to transact various services.
- There has to be a regulatory mechanism that comes in terms of providing or provisioning interoperability. So, there is a great opportunity for relevant stakeholders to start lobbying with the government and say create a standard.
- Till such time as interoperability doesn't come in, trade will not happen, remittances will not flow from one platform to the other platform. A poor rickshaw puller plying his rickshaw in Gurgaon will not be able to send his money back to Darbhanga because his platform doesn't understand the other platform and so on and so forth.
- Interoperability does not seem to be a big problem. But common platform is necessary. These two are different: common platform is necessary to reduce the cost, to speed up and scale up, but interoperability is not at all an issue as long as each technology provider is compatible with the concerned bank's core.
- Interoperability is not a big question and much of the energy is unnecessarily diverted towards that.
- Everybody is talking about standardised technology, while new technologies are emerging everyday.
- What is required now is to allow innovative experiments to flourish; do not look for any standardisation.
- When a new technology is created, ensure that the technology is created with an open standard.
- RBI is mandating that every solution has to be interoperable within six months time, so it is being taken care of.
- Interoperability should not be confined to one bank talking to another. Can a BC talk to the bank? Can the *gram panchayat* talk to the bank? These kinds of things will come in a very big way as computerisation is also catching up. In three years from now, it will be a reality and at that point in time one may have integration nightmare. So, from that context also this is very important.

- Interoperability is vitally important. Standardisation of anything but the interoperable interfaces is futile.
- The RBI, Ministry of IT and the Bureau of Indian Standards is still struggling with standardising so-called contact cards and contact-less cards and define the contents therein. They are outdated now.
- Interoperability need not be a big issue, but it must be ensured that it is not even a small issue by insisting that no technology shall be accepted by any end user unless the interfaces for incoming data and outgoing data and the commands to invoke those processes are made available to the purchaser of the technology.
- Any standardised technology is necessarily an old technology because standardisation process in this country takes two years and in that time, the technology has already been overtaken. This is not to say that old technology is not to be used, because old technology is mature. But, we need to evaluate every technology from the point of cost effectiveness.
- Interoperability may not be insisted upon at this stage.

Security Issues?

- Today if one goes to his bank, all he needs is to fill in a withdrawal slip and sign and the teller checks that handwritten signature which can be copied multiple times. That is the security on which the systems in this country have been working perfectly fine.
- Till the UID comes in to place, the voter ID may be made a common factor for exchanging the creditworthiness information.
- Once the fingerprints are taken, then the transparency and the general security are well taken care of.
- It is not a technology security issue. If there are any loopholes, it means that people (banks) are not investing properly into the security.
- As of now, security can be used very creatively and it can be absolutely binding. There are no impediments.
- There is a difference between the technology security issues and the business security issues.

Potential of Unique ID?

- There is an initiative, currently underway, in the government for issuing a unique identity to every individual. With that, the question of identity would become much simpler. Everyone will be identified, will have a unique number and there would be a national database with the names and identity numbers and photographs available which could be accessed by authorised people including financial sector institutions, and possibly over the next 3-4 years after that it will be biometric also. But there are still questions on what kind of an identification document, would it be on paper or would it be a card or would it be a smart card, etc. These questions are primarily because there is a cost attached to it. A simple calculation shows that even if it is Rs. 100 a card, we are talking about Rs. 10,000 crore just for the card. It is quite a large sum of money just for giving a card.
- UID is an enabler for financial institutions.
- Swiss Banks do business only on the basis of the account number. Why is it then we insist on everything and unless everything is in place, no transaction will be permitted? It is in this context that one requires a unique identifier for every Indian citizen.
- Unless there is a unique ID for a person, it is extremely difficult to cross-sterilise creditworthiness information.
- Already national ID initial pilots have gone through government institutions like ITIs and BELs and all that. They have gone very successfully and now they are just finalising on what they want to go ahead with.
- There are several concerns around the unique ID in terms of what should be the unique ID, what should be the modality and the methodology of it.

Mobiles, Smart Cards and Contact Less Cards?

- If a person has a mobile phone and backend servers at the banks, one does not need any other physical product.
- Mobile phone is reaching the customers much more rapidly than

envisaged and one will see even the poorest having a mobile phone in the next 2-3 years.

- The maximum number of transactions in any financial system happens between citizens and merchants or citizens and citizens. A majority of these are completely outside the purview of the digital transaction system; they happen through cash. Cash is the most interoperable and most important common platform today. And the entire system is geared towards handling cash and effectively reaching cash fast. If one had digital cash, one need not push the cash at the remote test place. There is no doubt, therefore, that going forward things will not scale and become profitable unless one eventually converts all transactions into digital transactions. It will not be possible to say that one will have digital transactions up to this part but beyond this it has to be cash.
- There is about Rs. 15,000 crore available under the USO fund. If that USO fund could actually be diverted into giving a SIM card to each and every citizen, giving him a unique number, that is an idea.
- ATMs, mobile payment settlements, prepaid cards are all urban centric. It has nothing to do with rural poor and financial inclusion.
- The only thing needed in rural areas, is a SIM card for someone who has a phone, and you are set.

What Should be the Usage of Financial Inclusion Technology Fund?

- Innovations can be funded by the Financial Technology Fund.
- Every individual proposal is being debated by an advisory committee which has been set up consisting of Central government representatives, bankers, RBI and NABARD. All go through it in detail, and the process time is very long. Little disbursements have happened against the fund. There seem to be process as well as capacity issues both in making use of the fund.
- The money that was promised in the budget in 2007 has not been transferred to NABARD as yet. Only a token amount is currently available.

- Larger ICT companies should play a more proactive role in financial inclusion.

Looking Ahead

- One has to be practical on the ground. Ninety per cent of the accounts will not be active as even in the normal banking business 90 per cent of the accounts are not active. It will take some time. For more than 60 years, these people are financially excluded and today with a bank account, it cannot be expected from them to operate the account daily starting today. It will take at least 4-5 years for them to develop that habit. They need to be told repeatedly for two or three years and then only they will start. Now at least 10-15 per cent has started operating the account.
- After the cost benefit and user behaviour analysis it is found that it is not the households which are unwilling to open the account, it is the banks and the state government who are not in a position to provide the right environment.
- As long as the government says "We want to encourage competition but there has to be some regulation. One has to get some approvals, but we are going to be very proactive, we are going to listen to you, we are going to turn things around very quickly, and if you don't like something we will go back to the drawing board." There may be single window for fast clearances and let it be made national news.
- If financial inclusion is declared as one of the national priorities, achieving this by 2013, i.e., when it is time to elect the next Lok Sabha, is entirely doable. Like in the telecom sector where a lot has been done with no subsidies involved. So if one were to look at a person's financial wallet or how much they are willing to spend on financial services, the amount that they are willing to spend or need to spend is far more than what they are willing to spend on communication services. If this can be done in telecom, why can't it be done in financial services?
- If the government were to declare that it is a time bound national priority, the amount of money that would flow in spite of the regulation will solve the viability issue.

- Unless steps are taken on the demand side, i.e., in the real sectors, mere supply side solutions will not solve the problem. Credit is necessary for this but not sufficient. Credit has to be integrated and become a part of an overall programme aimed at improving the productivity and income of small farmers and other poor households. Putting in place an appropriate credit delivery system to meet the needs of all marginal and small farmers must go hand in hand with the efforts to improve the productivity of such farm households. So, it is extremely important that we integrate the credit delivery system of the organised financial system with the programmes and policies which are being initiated by the government in order to improve the lot of the poor.
- Even identity can actually be packaged into the mobile. So then, there is no longer talk about the cost of issuing an identity card, it is a part of enabling a person to do a whole lot of other things. It is incidental so it is not just a cost line. It is a part of operating expenses. So, once again there is a possibility of combining not just mobile and financial services but mobile, financial services and identity related services.
- Today with technology enabler, a bank branch can be in everybody's pocket. Suppose there are 200 million mobiles, it means there are 200 million bank branches. One can send money, receive money, remit money, and one can deposit money. May be within 5-10 years that will become true.

7 Conclusion and Recommendations

> RBI intends a migrant labourer from Bihar who is in Amritsar doing some work who has not a shred of paper on him, absolutely nothing by way of ID, his account should be opened for financial inclusion. That is the aim of financial inclusion.
>
> *Participant at Skoch Research Meeting*

Calculations of the cost of providing financial access to 111.55 million households using plastic cards amount to Rs .13,304 million. Given this, the Rs. 10,000 million provisioned as FITF and FIPF was more than enough to take care of the issue, if disbursed. As an aside, some people tend to compare this figure with Rs. 700,000 million of farm loan waiver which they classify as the cost of financial exclusion.

All the costs were based on what the banks are actually paying to vendors (BCs). By all accounts, these costs are unsustainable in the short to medium term for the BCs. The gap at the end of two years (using plastic cards) is Rs. 26.25 per account (refer Table 4.8—Chap 4). This gap of Rs. 26.25 is moreover applicable only in the case of AP where a transaction fee of 2 per cent is being paid. In other cases, the gap widens to Rs. 73.45 per account and full coverage of 111.55 million households would require a gap funding of Rs. 8193.35 million. Where a transaction fee is paid, the gap would be Rs. 2928.19 million.

Admittedly, there has been some movement forward in as much as 25.15 million no-frills accounts have been opened. But, only 11 per cent are live accounts, so it is debatable how much financial inclusion has been achieved! In other words, only 2.77 million more households have a bank account that they use. This is only 2.48 per cent of the 111.55 million excluded households.

The following shortcomings in the current efforts were identified:

1. Not-for-profit mandate for providing financial access makes it a non-starter.

2. Fund availability, institutional empowerment as well as institutional capacity to manage/disburse the FITF.
3. Mission mode approach and operations are missing.
4. If the largest PSU banks decided to take on the cost of financial inclusion, the overall figure at Rs. 2,660 million per year, over a five-year period, is so insignificant compared to their balance sheets that financial inclusion would have happened many times over. Instead, the entire burden has been passed on to the littlest and the poorest link in the chain, the BC.
5. Regulated interest rates even at the bottom of the pyramid where these are clearly unsustainable due to transaction costs and risk profiles. No wonder, lending activity in these accounts is also not happening.
6. No provisioning for a reasonable transaction fee for handling social payments like NREGS by the Central government.
7. BCs are not viewed as an extension to the banks, either by the banks or by the customers resulting in poor availability of services and even poorer offtake thereof.
8. The belief in the mythical revenue from other services that could help BCs break even and the BC business being just an incremental revenue stream. This myth has been broken in several similar projects, including some in the e-governance space. This is because of the following reasons:
   a) The end customer is a marginalised entity, surviving on the fringes, and food security is his major concern. Expecting any other remunerative consumption is a bit unrealistic.
   b) If monopoly services like banking and governance cannot be sustainable on their own merit, there is little hope for anything else that is free market to become sustainable.
9. There is a misplaced optimism about specified individual category BCs and NGOs taking financial inclusion to scale. What is often forgotten is the cost of enrolling, training, managing and keeping effective thousands of retired government servants and school teachers, etc. Banks who have done so successfully in pilots have, however, not managed to scale. The most cost-effective option of

managing such a channel still seems to be through the intermediary BC (organisation).

10. Restrictions on who can be a BC or can render micro-financial services is limiting outreach, thereby undermining the goal of universal financial access.
11. Financial literacy is simply not happening.
12. The perception of financial inclusion varies with the change in the state government. Bhamasha project, currently in abeyance in Rajasthan is a case in point.

There is need for an attitudinal change, there is need for a change in organisational structure and there is need for innovative models of delivery at the doorstep. Financial inclusion is no longer an option, it is a compulsion.[1]

The learning curve in the process of inclusive growth has shown that the time is right to promote integration of common services and platforms to widen their coverage. Provision of financial services to rural communities, especially poor communities, has traditionally focused on extending credit. The need for providing effective training facilities, financial advice and insurance, especially against the failure of their livelihood activity, was largely ignored. Today, the need is for such facilities. These needs take precedence over the need for credit because it improves clients' ability to smooth consumption with their own resources without carrying the burden of debt during income downswings. However, the only difference is that structure or nature of products required or delivery mechanisms may differ in rural areas.

The business of being a BC seems viable in the long term but not in the short and medium term. Like many other businesses, the BC also requires an initial financing support from a bank or some other entity (NABARD/ Government). The BCs, for some reasons difficult to pinpoint, are not being provided this financial support, and are instead expected to become investors to set up the basic infrastructure for financial inclusion in villages.

Equally unclear still is the role of the FI funds. The Finance Minister in his budget for 2007-08 has announced the setting up of two funds

---

1. Rangarajan, C. (2007). *Financial Inclusion: Some Key Issues*. Lecture delivered at Mangalore University, Mangalore, August 10.

for FI; the first called Financial Inclusion Fund for developmental and promotional interventions and the other called Financial Inclusion Technology Fund to meet cost of technology adoption of about Rs. 5000 million each. The initial contribution of GoI has been only to the extent of Rs.100 million for each of the funds. NABARD has contributed Rs. 50 million each. But till date, NABARD the lead agency in this regard is yet to come out with clear project areas or guidelines.

The Committee on Financial Inclusion has already outlined the basic strategy for building an inclusive financial sector in terms of four components:[2]

- Effecting improvements within the existing formal credit delivery mechanism;
- Suggesting measures for improving credit absorption capacity, especially amongst marginal and sub-marginal farmers and poor non-cultivator households;
- Evolving new models for effective outreach; and
- Leveraging on technology-based solutions.

This study sought to collate views from all stakeholders (backed by primary research and further triangulated through a community e-discussion) so as to arrive at key interventions and intermediations to speed up the process of financial inclusion, and thereby poverty alleviation in the country. The recommendations outline different options for solving some of the issues identified above.

Strategies must ensure that at least one member in family should have one bank account in next 3-5 years. The discussions and analyses formulated three new goals that marry the twin aims of financial and social inclusion:

- Everyone should be able to manage their money effectively and securely, through having access to a bank account, and the confidence and capability to get the most from it.
- Everyone should be able to plan for the future with a reasonable degree of certainty. Therefore, affordable credit, savings accounts and simple insurance products should be available to all who need them.

---

2. "Report of the Committee on Financial Inclusion," Economic Advisory Council to the Prime Minister, Government of India, January 2008.

- Everyone should have the information, support and confidence they need to prevent avoidable financial difficulty, and to know where to turn if they do find themselves in financial distress.

The onus is clearly on the government to create legal space and improve the financial regulatory system to facilitate integration of financial services for the poor into the mainstream of finance. The key recommendation that emerge from this study are:

Key Recommendations

Financial Inclusion Should be Declared a National Priority

The Report of the Committee on Financial Inclusion suggested that a National Rural Financial Inclusion Plan (NRFIP) be launched in mission mode with a clear target to provide access to comprehensive financial services, including credit, to at least 50 per cent (say 55.77 million) of the financially excluded cultivator/non-cultivator households, by 2012. It is recommended that the mission should also include urban poor and Micro, Small and Medium Enterprises (MSMEs). For the purpose, a National Mission on Financial Inclusion (NaMFI) should be constituted comprising representatives from all stakeholders to aim at achieving universal financial access in the medium term and universal financial inclusion in the long term. The proposed mission should be entrusted with managing and disbursing the FITF and FIPF, besides more such funds should be created for tackling urban poverty.

The banks may be mandated to take up the cost of universal financial access as part of their business obligation. Alternatively they should contribute a percentage of their turnover to a 'Universal Financial Access Fund' (UFAF) to be managed by the mission. While the idea is borrowed from the Universal Services Obligation Fund (USOF) of the telecom sector, the mission-mode institutional mechanism would perhaps deliver better results than the USOF.

The poor performance of banks in the Differential Rate of Interest (DRI) Scheme has been of concern to policy makers. It is suggested here that the funds under the DRI Scheme may be utilised for lending in financial inclusion initiatives. This will

- provide free funds for lending,
- provide cheaper funds for MFIs and BCs for onward lending, and
- micro credit would see greater linkages with livelihoods.

The mission may be entrusted with the task of monitoring the DRI Scheme. Projects like Bhamasha should be encouraged as they offer scale. They could even be made into a national scheme for BPL women and be handled by the Mission.

Review BC/BF Model

The following recommendations are in the nature of options identified for making the BC model viable and more effective.

1. Access to venture funding

   The following measures are recommended:

   a) Removal of the 10 per cent cap on corporate holding in a BC.

   b) Removal of BC as a not-for profit company conditionality. If this is likely to create some major regulatory problems, then the banks themselves should invest in BCs. This, however, can repeat the RRB experience wherein the BC employees would at some juncture want to be treated at par with bank employees, negating the lower cost advantage.

2. Funding the viability gap

   The following measures are recommended:

   a) The FIPF Fund should be utilised immediately to compensate BCs for the viability gap.

   b) Adequate transaction fee (based on the cost structures described in this report) for NREGA and other social benefit payments should be provided for and made mandatory by the Centre. Eighty-five per cent of this should be for the BC and 15 per cent would go to the bank.

   c) Banks could proactively engage the BCs in loan services, including recovery (at say, a recovery fee of 20 per cent for NPAs that have been written off in the books of the bank), insurance, etc. The business case is strengthened only if existing direct accounts (SHG, no-frill, micro credit, GCC-linked) opened by the bank are handed over to BCs, thereby making the BC an extension service of the bank. This would not only lessen NPAs in this regard but do so in a cost-effective way for the banks.

d) The banks could provide long-term loans at priority sector interest rates without collateral (on the basis of projected 5-year balance sheets) to meet the working capital needs of BCs. The software export industry enjoys something like this in a limited way.

e) As an option, the banks could foot the entire bill of infrastructure and technology and also pay service charges and transaction fee to the BCs. This can be recouped by the bank in the following ways:

- Augmentation of loans and deposits' business volumes.
- End-user charges on transactions and accounts, collected on behalf of the bank by the BC. This should take into account the cost structures given in the Andhra model (Refer Table 4.6, Chapter 4). Today, the financial inclusion guidelines from RBI prohibit the banks from charging the end user any fee for any service. This inhibits banks from investing resources.
- Allowing banks to charge an interest rate in the band of PLR+5 per cent for loans below Rs. 200,000. This will also spur credit disbursement.

3. Widening the definition of BCs as well as thinking outside the BC model to incorporate other channels that are already pervasive at the last mile. For example, CSCs, telcos, PCO operators, Panchayati Raj Institutions, etc.
4. NBFCs engaged in microfinance activities should be recognised as a separate institution.

The BC scheme was originally intended to provide greater reach to the banks at a reasonable cost. However, now we find that banks are looking at the viability of the scheme strictly based on what respective state governments are willing to pay for electronic benefits transfer! This is not possible as a BC would be severely underutilised if restricted to only EBT payments. Further, a breakeven cannot be achieved with such low capacity utilisation. The viability would come from introduction of other products and services that a bank does through the BC instead of its own staff.

Towards Greater Financial Literacy

For sustaining financial inclusion, financial literacy becomes a very critical component. There is a need to simultaneously focus on the financial literacy part besides delivery/access. The following measures are recommended:

- Education campaigns to showcase banking services advantages and how to use them.
- Provide training packages at CSCs and other e-kiosks.
- Utilise Panchayati Raj Institutions to mobilise the people.
- Greater role for NGOs.
- Inculcate financial literacy at school itself. Present day school pass-outs need to be a lot more financially literate than their parents were, if they are to manage their personal finances successfully through life.
- Lead banks should open a Financial Literacy and Credit Counselling Centre (FLCC) in every district, where they have lead responsibility. This has already been suggested but now needs to be implemented and the same monitored.
- FLCCs may be linked to the RUDSETIs—Rural Development & Self Employment Training Institutes, which are providing micro-enterprise training.

Overcoming Regional Imbalances

Regional imbalances in the financial inclusion process are quite visible. Household access to financial services varies widely across states in ways that are not correlated with income and there is a need to broadbase the effort to make financial inclusion more meaningful and inclusive.

- Develop clear indicators of the extent of the financial exclusion problem and be able to assess the efficiency measures implemented and their impact on financial exclusion.
- Branch managers are currently not given any incentive to act on such accounts as it is not profitable in the short run. While incentives are purely based on profit one brings to the bank, banks should think of providing incentives to schemes that promote social inclusion.

- Strengthen SHG-Bank linkage: This can be regarded as one of the most potent initiatives for delivering financial services to the poor. The inclusiveness of SHG-Bank linkage, which has involved a partnership between government, NGOs and a range of rural banks (commercial banks, RRBs, cooperative banks) has already given good results. One of the distinctive features of the SHG-Bank linkage programme has been the high recovery rate. However, the spread of SHGs is very uneven and is more concentrated in southern states. This regional imbalance needs to be corrected and special efforts in this regard may have to be taken by NABARD. As suggested by the Committee on Financial Inclusion, NABARD be given additional powers to supervise the SHGs that may be established in the urban areas also. The possibility of the SHGs becoming effective organisations in the urban areas is there and therefore, we should explore this particular possibility. SHGs also need to graduate from mere providers of credit for non-productive purposes to promoting micro enterprises.
- Special focus on North-east region: This region has the highest percentage of people who are financially excluded and the number of urban bank branches, number of rural bank branches, number of cooperatives or post offices are also very less. Special initiatives are required to bring this area into the mainstream. A common technology infrastructure for financial inclusion should be put up as 100 per cent funded through the FITF.

Target Needs and Product Innovation

- Penetration of insurance services: Insurance services largely remain as the urban phenomena. It should reach out to the rural and remote areas and to the poor segments of the societies. Micro insurance services should be given greater importance while extending financial services
- Encourage Bancassurance: Bancassurance—a term coined by combining the two words bank and insurance—connotes distribution of insurance products through banking channels. As financial inclusion would involve access to both, bank as well as insurance, increasing bancassurance would help. The challenges ahead of

bancassurance are mostly regulatory. The broad areas are, one determining common acceptable standards that can qualify a banker to get involved in insurance and two, sharing of the fee/commission structure between the bank and the insurance company.

- Coupling government assistance with formal banking system may increase financial inclusion better than just offering people accounts. The channelling of NREGA payments through banks and post offices has seen positive results.
- There is a need for public policy intervention for improvement of financial services in urban areas, especially focused on remittances for migrant labourers.
- Utilisation of DRI Scheme: Under DRI Scheme banks are required to achieve the targets of one per cent of the aggregate advances prescribed for the entire country. "The Committee are unhappy to observe that the overall performance of banks under DRI Scheme continues to lag behind the targeted level. The main reason advanced for the banks' failure to achieve the target is the preference of the targeted groups for subsidy linked programmes. Repeated advice to the banks by RBI to improve their performance under the DRI Scheme has had little effect. In fact, their performance has declined year after year during the last six years. The Committee desire that concerted efforts need to be made by the banks to improve their performance under the DRI Scheme. As the entire responsibility of the implementation of the scheme vests with the banks, the Ministry of Finance should not remain a mute spectator to the poor performance of the banks under the DRI Scheme."[3]

The Committee did not not share the perception of the Ministry that Differential Rate of Interest (DRI) Scheme is not attractive enough and the beneficiaries prefer subsidy linked schemes. In view of the concessional rate of interest of 4 per cent per annum on finance provided under DRI Scheme, it should have been more attractive to the weaker sections of the society. The Committee notes that the entire responsibility of implementation of the Scheme vests with the banks. Hence, the initiative for identifying eligible beneficiaries and assessing their suitability and viability should come from the banks.

---

3. GoI Estimate Committee Observation/Recommendation (Sl. No. 7, Para No. 1.118)

As on the December 31, 2008, the aggregate advance level under DRI scheme was Rs. 108.12 crore against Rs. 33.25 crore as of March 2008. In terms of national benchmark, the level of advances under DRI as of December 2008 accounts for only 0.49 per cent of the total advances (Rs. 22,077.23 crore) as on March 31, 2008, against the target of one per cent of total credit. As per the Union Finance Minister's directives, all banks have been requested to finance at least 10 beneficiaries per branch under the scheme. It is recommended, therefore, that the unutilised amount be used for advancing small loans under the financial inclusion initiative. This upholds the spirit of the DRI scheme and also provides loans at cheaper rates for weaker sections. This should be used for microcredit and establishing livelihood linkages.

Leverage Existing Technology

To make banking services available to everyone, technology has to be leveraged to create channels beyond branch network to reach the un-banked all over the country. This is even more true of the existing technology infrastructure where there are no additional capital costs and the rollout can be immediate.

- e-Kiosks in villages could be a source of operating a remittance system.[4] In this regard, utilising the 100,000 Common Services Centres (CSCs) set up under the National e-Governance Plan (NeGP) may be allowed. These will function like common facilitation centre, a point at which the citizen can avail services of varied nature. If correctly implemented, the scheme would serve to reduce costs, improve efficiencies and significantly broaden the bouquet of services currently available to the country's rural population.
- Mobile telephony can provide the last-mile connectivity for financial inclusion in partnerships with banks. While mobile banking is not a new concept, the public banks themselves seem to be lacking the marketing savvy and the initiative to make it popular even in urban areas, therefore rural areas would be a long haul. This can be compared with the success of value-added services being directly provided by telcos.

---

4. "Report of the Committee on Financial Inclusion," Economic Advisory Council to the Prime Minister, Government of India, January 2008, p. 20.

- The fastest way to speed up universal financial access is perhaps to piggyback on the existing mobile operators. There was an opinion that if telcos are directly allowed to handle financial transactions (limited by number of transactions, amounts, etc.), there can be a balance between regulatory needs and speed and scale of implementation. This requires consideration and further examination.
- The concept of pocket banking needs to be revisited and guidelines defined once the UID has been implemented. Pocket banking would utilise the UID and mobile telephony to achieve greater financial inclusion and social empowerment. This would also help in removing regional imbalances. We can provide technology to the, say, remote corners of Arunachal Pradesh where mobiles are charged using solar technology but how do we get cash there is a really big challenge. The only real solution may be to do barter using cashless mode of transaction through mobiles.
- There was consensus that the UID will be an enabler for financial inclusion. A provision of Rs. 100 crore in the Annual Plan 2009-10 has already been made for a Unique Identification Authority of India. Linkage with financial services should be explored from the very beginning. It may be noted that pilot projects to provide smart cards have not been very cost effective. It is perhaps not an option best suited for a single application usage.
- Encourage multi-bank platforms which can communicate with each other to enable a nationwide affordable remittance system.

Revamping of RRBs and Cooperative Banks

The nearly 50,000 rural/semi-urban cooperative bank branches also have to increase their accessibility to small and marginal farmers and other poorer segments. Regulation and supervision of these banks needs to be urgently strengthened.

- Prudential regulation standards related to capital adequacy, asset classification, income recognition and provisioning need to be upgraded and introduced in a phased manner, and the supervisory enforcement improved. At the same time, this would need to be accompanied by operational restructuring, involving improvements in governance to reduce state interference, better management, staffing policies that allow banks to employ local staff who are familiar with the community and thereby better able to address the needs of their client, and the introduction of new products, such as loans with flexible repayment terms, and better services, such as door-step banking that can help better to meet the needs of rural clients and minimise risk.

- It has been suggested that the IDRBT could offer interest free loans to UCBs and RRBs for adoption of IT instead of looking at FITF for this.
- RRBs may also usefully adopt the business facilitator and business correspondent model to achieve greater inclusion.

Apart from the RRBs and cooperative banks, the aims of financial inclusion can also be addressed by MFIs, NGOs, postal system and various other channels. These have been addressed separately by the Rangarajan Committee on Financial Inclusion and several recommendations were made for each. Upon examination, we agree with the Committee's recommendations and urge that these be implemented at the earliest. We have already pointed out the need to widen the definition of BCs as well.

Promote and Encourage Research

It is becoming increasingly apparent that addressing financial exclusion will require a holistic approach on the part of the banks in creating awareness about financial products, education, and advice on money management, debt counselling, savings and affordable credit. The banks will have to evolve specific strategies to expand the outreach of their services in order to promote financial inclusion. One of the ways in which this can be achieved in a cost-effective manner is through forging linkages with microfinance institutions and local communities. Action research needs to be undertaken to explore the possibilities as follows:

- Finding out appropriate institutions which can serve as a good link between the commercial banks, rural branches and the farm households. One subject for such research could be village cooperative credit societies. These societies can also become facilitators or correspondents for the commercial banks. Several of the village level credit cooperative societies have reached their limits and are therefore, not in a position to be able to provide credit out of their own resources or out of the borrowed resources. In such cases, the village cooperative credit societies can act as a correspondent for the commercial banks.

- Electronic cash system seems to be the future. This would also overcome the cash management issue and help deepen both financial and digital inclusion. To this end, it is suggested that a pilot study be undertaken by Skoch Development Foundation, financially supported by NABARD, in 20-25 villages to set up an electronic cash payment system using a multi-purpose card. NABARD was amenable to the suggestion at the national consultation meet.

The poor need banking services for channelising their small surpluses and to link to institutional service for those who still depend on informal sources of savings. For accelerated growth of the economy, it is necessary that all the people should be covered by the sector through financial inclusion. It is not the agenda of the bank alone. Financial inclusion is a collective effort. It is an agenda in which everyone has a role, either as a user or as a partner. When we look at the recommendations of the Rangarajan Committee or the Raghuraman Committee, they propose a paradigm shift in the way we see the financial inclusion. The committee wants there should be a reason for expanding financial services such as savings products, insurance products and inflation-protected ventures. The committee strongly recommends the national goal of ensuring within three years access to a deposit account to at least 90 per cent of the households if they so desire, and to the payment system and the various schemes implemented through this system. Currently, most banks are satisfied with just opening of no-frills accounts and promptly announce that 100 per cent financial inclusion has been achieved. They should go one step further and make available the needed financial services i.e., credit, remittance or insurance as the case may be, to the underserved/unserved segments, so that universal financial access takes place in the true sense.

Access to finance is clearly not purely a financial sector issue; hence, financial sector measures alone can resolve it. Access to finance has social and other non-financial dimensions. Poor and low income households suffer from multiple, often inter-locking, disadvantages. Because of this, many other measures are also needed to address this issue effectively, such as improvements to education, rural infrastructure, primary health care and other vital services. There is need for capacity building and governance reforms to go hand in hand with financial inclusion.

Unless and until the government and the financial sector work together, financial inclusion cannot happen because it is more of a governance issue and less of a financial issue. The proportion is very dependent on whom you are talking to, but unless and until the 80,000 crore of social spending that India does, is better targeted to the end recipient through the banking system as a second level check of leakages on one hand and an instrument to capture at least some savings on the other. Deepening the financial system and widening its reach is crucial for both accelerating growth and for equitable distribution, given the present stage of development of our country. The key however, lies in linking access to financial services with livelihood options and leveraging the same to achieve poverty eradication.

8 Case Studies

Bank of Baroda

Bank of Baroda has adopted the 'whole village approach' as part of its mandate for enabling for financial inclusion by extending banking services to the country's rural population. This though is not a new initiative for the Bank, since the passion for agriculture and rural development is ingrained in the Bank's philosophy since its inception in 1908. To give rural India access to finance and to enable economic independence, BoB has introduced a slew of services that extend credit facilities to small and marginal farmers, agricultural labourers and cottage industry entrepreneurs. Villages in Dungarpur district of Rajasthan were among the first 500 villages to benefit from the bank's financial inclusion and total integrated village development programme.

In the past too, the Bank has taken a number of initiatives such as opening of specialised outlets of Gram Vikas Kendras (GVKs) and Multi Service Agencies (MSAs). The Baroda Swarojgar Vikas Sansthan (BSVS) was another initiative for capacity building and provided appropriate training for skill upgradation to unemployed youth and women for employment.

The Baroda Kisan Credit Card (BKCC) is yet another facility offered by the bank to empower the farmer. The credit card designed exclusively for the benefit of the farmers aims to provide them the opportunity to manage and utilise their funds in the manner they deem fit. The Kisan Credit Card provides adequate and timely support to farmers for their production needs, which include among others, purchase of quality inputs, investment requirements like purchase of agriculture implements/tractor etc., farming expenses towards farm maintenance, unforeseen family expenses and maintenance of non-farm activities.

As part of the Bank's commitment to corporate social responsibility in its centenary year, i.e., 2007-08, BoB launched the Baroda Grameen

Paramarsh Kendra (BGPK)—a centre for knowledge sharing, problem solving and credit counselling for the rural communities. The BGPK is an effort to narrow the "knowledge gap" in financial literacy, better farming practices and technology adoption. It offers rural communities a diversity of opportunities including market-linked prices, value addition services offered by various institutions, women empowerment and employment opportunities for rural youth.

The BGPK centre helps in spreading financial awareness among rural masses through village level meetings and helps them to choose suitable banking products. As part of information sharing and problem solving process, it holds interface sessions with the specialists from institutions like agriculture universities, Kisan Vikas Kendras and NGOs working in the rural development sector. The centre also provides extension services to the farmers by encouraging their participation in *grameen melas*, and organising television and radio talks. Each of the BGVK centre also maintains a small library containing books, journals and audio-visual aids. Information on the prices of agriculture commodities in various mandis across the country is also provided, enabling the farmers to sell their products at the best prices. The farmers are also provided credit counselling on repayment pattern and rescheduling of loans and fresh credit during situations of rural distress.

Another important initiative is the Baroda Kisan Group Loan—a joint liability scheme—for purchase of heavy agricultural machinery like tractors, power-tillers, etc., either by farmers having larger holdings with irrigation facilities or group of farmers with irrigation facilities. The bank also provides credit for purchase of second hand tractors to farmers interested in dry-land farming or having a small land holding. Production credit is also provided for raising various crops from the point of preparatory tillage till harvesting, for landowners or permanent tenants or leaseholders or sharecroppers. It encourages the development of irrigation facilities; this covers sinking of wells/bore wells, lifting of water by installation of pump sets, transporting of water through field channels, water saving systems like drip irrigation/sprinkler irrigation etc., for farmers. It also extends working capital to dealers/distributors/traders of agricultural inputs like seeds, fertilisers, livestock inputs like cattle feed, medicine etc., and supply of agriculture machinery/irrigation systems.

Employment is provided to the unemployed technical personnel through the Agro Service Centre. The bank also facilitates the setting up of agri-clinics and agri-business centres by agriculture graduates. To address the needs of rural infrastructure, the bank provides credit for the construction of farm building/structures like cattle sheds, thrashing yards, fencing etc., to the individual farmer or firms engaged in agricultural activity and is of long term nature. Credit is also provided for construction/expansion/modernisation/renovation of rural godowns and cold storages.

Other services provided by the bank include, development of horticulture including production, processing and marketing of various fruit, vegetables, plantations and flowers, from the nursery to the point of market, by individual farmers, firms, organisations like cooperative societies. A number of allied activities, like dairy, poultry, fisheries, sericulture, mushrooms and apiculture are also encouraged by the bank. To ensure financial inclusion for the Scheduled Caste and Scheduled Tribes who have been provided/allotted land by the state government, the bank finances their purchase of farm implements, irrigation systems and bullocks etc.

The bank has also allied itself with NGOs to encourage the formation of credit linked SHGs in the villages. Under the Dungarpur Project, the bank works through the People's Education and Development Organisation (PEDO), a NGO working in rural development.

This initiative of the bank has already brought about a change in the lives of people. Bank of Baroda has also announced plans of adopting more villages across the country. It plans to disburse credit worth Rs. 1 billion, over the next three years in these villages. Of these, 'Baroda Centenary Villages', as they will be called, 25 will be in Gujarat. The bank will also spend Rs. 5 million to 7.5 million on these 25 villages for their social development. This will be done in consultation with the *panchayats* and other voluntary bodies.

Canara Bank

Over 48 Canara Gramin Vikas Vahinis fan out to villages across the country every day under the Canara Bank's financial inclusion initiative. After undergoing intensive training, the staff of rural and semi-urban branches use these vehicles to meet villagers at their doorstep, explain the various extension products and services and then bring them into the banking fold. Accounts are opened instantly and loans sanctioned on the spot.

Canara Bank has adopted technology and co-developed biometric voice enabled smart cards along with the technology provider. The bank has also engaged the services of business correspondents who are able to reach out to the villages with handheld devices. In fact, the smart card has brought banking to the doorsteps of the villagers.

Financial inclusion is an important corporate goal of Canara Bank. Mobile voice-based ATMs, seven of which now operate nationwide, are part of the drive. The mobile ATM consists of a bus which has a voice-enabled, biometric money vending machine. The ATM accepts only the customer's fingerprint as password and also guides the customer to withdraw money through recorded voice instructions in the local language. These features make this ATM especially useful to cater to an illiterate clientele.

The bank is also assisting village artisans like blacksmiths, carpenters, leather workers, people engaged in servicing of agricultural implements and household equipments. In addition, the bank also has 36 training centres of which 14 impart training in special skills so as provide rural youth with opportunities for self-employment. The bank also provides loan for setting up of such businesses.

It has also helped set up several women self-help groups (SHGs) and is providing training and other supports to empower the women and improve livelihood opportunities. Taking products to the market has always been a challenge for rural artisans. Recognising this, Canara Bank has provided a vehicle to the SHG with barcode facility so that they can take their products to areas of demand for sell. The vehicle doubles up as a sales counter facilitating easy movement between points of sale.

It is not surprising then that Canara Bank is also extremely proactive on the CSR front as well. It has provided financial support for the construction of schools in over 100 villages at an average of Rs. 1 lakh per school. It has also adopted 23 villages across the country where it has sought to upgrade infrastructure by providing roads, health care facilities, etc.

Corporation Bank

Establishing banks at every village is not possible—it demands immense funds and huge workforce. The answer Corporation Bank has found is to go in for 'branchless banking'. It has used this model successfully in Chittoor district of Andhra Pradesh to bring more villages under financial inclusion in unbanked areas. The key to making this a success is linking banking with livelihood. According to the bank, financial inclusion is of no use if it fails to provide livelihood to the poor. With the help of technology, the poor need to be brought into the mainstream of growth.

In a joint project with National Dairy Development Board (NDDB), it has launched Milk Mitra cards in Chittoor district. Under this, women milk producers are given loans to enter dairy farming, the milk is supplied to NDDB and all payments are made directly to the bank account of each woman. These accounts can be accessed at the village level itself through the business correspondent, also a member of the local community.

It is a classic case of business at the bottom of the pyramid—and where commercial and social responsibilities can converge This is clear if one looks at the successful implementation of the Milk Mitra card. The milk card scheme has also been replicated with the help of smart card for other produce also, like vegetables and flowers.

In fact, in Chittoor district, the Corporation Bank has added yet another dimension to this model, keeping in view the *mantra* of linking banking with livelihoods. It has been seen over time that branchless banking and better livelihood opportunities have inculcated the habit of saving in the villages. It's clearly a win-win situation for both the bank and the people!

Such schemes have yet another positive spin-off. The section of the rural population that has benefited the most from these schemes is the women. They have grabbed the opportunity to not only add to their family's finances but also have invested in their self-esteem. The money they earn goes directly to their account and they can thus, use it judiciously. The challenge for the bank was to take the more sophisticated technology to unsophisticated areas, as most of the rural areas are short of power and telephone connectivity. Added to this, the rural populace is not familiar with complicated machine operations.

Under the branchless banking model, basic banking services are provided without having to open an expensive branch. Each identified person is given a smart card which is akin to e-purse. One of the villagers is appointed as "business correspondent" and he or she is given the branchless banking kit and cash to dispense basic banking services to the villagers. The kit is a handheld device with multiple connectivity options. The operations are carried out through radio frequency identification cards provided to business correspondents and the villagers. So, the model not only provides banking services to the villagers, it also opens an employment opportunity.

This model has yet another benefit. With the smart card, one can deposit or withdraw (money) at their own convenience. Additionally, there is no requirement to fill any forms or vouchers, which is quite useful for the illiterate segment that the scheme is seeking to target. The services are made available close to their homes, obviating the need to spend time and money on transport to reach the branch. The roll out and maintenance costs of this model are only a fraction of running a conventional branch.

This system is now proving to be a role model. Indian Institute of Management, Ahmedabad has evinced keen interest in the "Branchless Banking" model evolved by the bank, which takes technology to the remotest villages of the country for providing banking facility. On its part, the Corporation Bank plans to extend this model to all villages in the country.

LIC—Jeevan Madhur

Recognising that insurance products had a distinctly urban bias, Life Insurance Corporation of India (LIC) took up the challenge of developing unique insurance products specifically directed towards rural India: one that was affordable for its rural clients even as it was sustainable for the institution.

Jeevan Madhur micro-insurance policy, launched by LIC in 2006, caters to the needs of the poor, both rural and urban, who cannot afford large premium of the conventional insurance sold through individual agents. An endowment policy, Jeevan Madhur not only gives death risk cover but also maturity benefit. The sum assured ranges from Rs. 5,000 to a maximum of Rs. 30,000 for a duration of 5 years up to 15 years.

It is especially targeted to cover the low-income group and especially those who have no fixed and stable income. Mode of payment of premium can be even weekly/fortnightly in addition to other regular modes to suit the needs of people with low income. Minimum premium is Rs. 25 per week, Rs. 50 per fortnight, Rs. 100 per month which is expected to be well within reach of the targeted group.

Jeevan Madhur, is available to both males and females without any medical examination and is a simple saving related life insurance plan covering individuals in the age group of 18 to 60 years.

The maturity benefit is in proportion to the amount of premium, term of policy and age of the life assured. The policy, if kept in full force, is entitled to the simple reversionary bonuses depending upon Corporation's experience. Accident benefit is also applicable as per terms and conditions of the policy. After premiums are paid for 2 years, auto cover facility i.e., continuance of cover even in case of inability to pay premium up to 2 years from the date of first unpaid premium, is available to take care of contingencies and uncertainties of income.

Micro-insurance is an important tool to provide a social net to the lower income families in our country and risk cover for small entrepreneurs and farmers. These people do not have any other means of securing their life and businesses.

Punjab National Bank

Tineri village, situated about 65 km from Patna under Masaurhi block of Patna district, came into the limelight after Punjab National Bank (PNB) decided to make it the centre of attraction as part of its drive to foster greater financial inclusion in the country. Here, PNB decided to set up its branchless banking facility to serve the poor who had no idea about the diversified banking services.

The Tineri project was part of the 27 pilot projects (20 in rural areas and 7 in urban areas) launched by PNB across 13 states in the Indo-Gangetic Belt. The objective was to cover the Indo-Gangetic plain, where the bank has more inherent strength, not only in terms of outreach but also infrastructure availability.

Importantly, a key partner in the Tineri project was the local Panchayati Raj Institution, which PNB felt was an essential to ensure the project's success. *Panchayats* have been key enablers, according to PNB, in motivating people to open accounts, the verification of which was undertaken by PNB. This was especially important when it came to motivating people to move away from traditional, but high-cost, lending sources like the money lender. PNB saw itself here as a catalytic agent, with an essential element here being peoples' participation.

The Tineri initiative was not only as part of PNB's social responsibility, but was also seen as a "holistic approach" towards providing basic banking facilities to the poorest of the poor in all corners of the country. The bank sees financial inclusion as a distinct opportunity and business proposition for future growth.

In Tineri and its surrounding 12 villages today, financial inclusion as per PNB's directive is complete, with all residents having opened bank accounts, with an overdraft facility. This has effectively ensured that local people do not go to the moneylender to raise funds and suffer exorbitant interest rates in the process.

Though this was a pilot project to access the acceptability of basic banking services to the remote villagers, most of whom are illiterate and have little or no idea about the value for money, PNB sees in it a new window of opportunity. Under the project, each family in Tineri and its surrounding villages is provided with a biometric card, a thermal filter and a Near Field Communication (NFC) mobile handset at a total cost of only Rs. 110. In return, each customer is allowed to open a savings bank account even with zero balance. Also, all transactions are made with the biometric card and the NFC. The technology employed here is a mobile-base technology, an instrument that enables the bank to open the account and do the transaction as well.

Importantly, all SHGs of Tineri are being imparted training for knowledge building and entrepreneurship programme under various sectors through RUDSETI Patna. The same is also being extended to Nadaul and Punpun *panchayats*. The bank's pilot projects show that two things have been done in Bihar. First, linking the people with the bank through the financial inclusion programme. Second, a tie-up which enables funding all the e-Seva Kendras through village level entrepreneurs. Such village level entrepreneurs will soon become individual business correspondents (BC) after due Reserve Bank of India verification. This will enable PNB cover 8,000 villages more.

To make PNB a household name in Bihar, the bank has also established an e-kiosk in each *panchayat* with the collaboration of SREI Infrastructure Finance Ltd. The first such project was launched in Panapur village. Besides providing other services as per the requirement of the *panchayat*, the kiosk operator or village level entrepreneur is seen working as a business facilitator for the bank for providing all types of banking services to the villagers. The success in Tineri has emboldened PNB to go ahead with its plans to bring about financial inclusion in Buxar, Rohtas, Gaya and Bhojpur districts of Bihar.

The Zero Platform

The Zero Platform has moved beyond pilot stage. Over 20,000 new accounts are opened every day now, across 18 states for the SBI family and a dozen other PSU and regional rural banks. Over 1 million unbanked citizens have been enrolled with their biometric data for no-frills accounts under the common network acceptance mark Zero, with accounts held across 21 different banks under the business correspondent model.

The BCs appointed by different banks to extend their outreach in villages through the Zero Platform include ZMF (Zero Microfinance and Savings Support Foundation); India Post (in an agreement with SBI); Drishtee Foundation; Indian Grameen Services (an affiliate of Basix); and many others.

The platform was first deployed in July 2006 for State Bank of India as the very first instance of the actual implementation of the business correspondent model, for extending SBI's outreach in Mizoram and Pithoragarh (Uttarakhand). After a trial period, the formal launch was made at a public function in Aizawl in Mizoram on November 7, 2006. This was followed quickly by a launch in Medak in Andhra Pradesh on November 19, 2006 and a month later in Pithoragarh in Uttarakhand on December.

The experience in the Medak District in Andhra Pradesh, six banks (State Bank of India, State Bank of Hyderabad, Andhra Pradesh Grameen Vikas Bank, Andhra Bank, Union Bank of India, Axis Bank) decided to back the Zero Platform for a landmark pilot in collaboration with the Government of Andhra Pradesh, under the active supervision of the RBI. This pilot was implemented in six *mandals* of Warangal District in Andhra Pradesh, to open no-frills accounts using biometric authentication for disbursal of social security pensions and wages under the National Rural Employment Guarantee Act (NREGA) to all beneficiaries in all villages that came within these 6 Mandals.

A Little World Pvt. Ltd. (ALW) provided the necessary technology and back-end services for the platform, while ZMF provided the last mile operations as a business correspondent to all the six banks in the pilot. ZMF was the first and is today the largest business correspondent to banks as part of the Reserve Bank of India's liberalised guidelines for financial inclusion. Today, 21 banks, including the State Bank of India and most of its subsidiaries, utilise the ZERO network based on NFC mobile phones and biometric authentication of customers.

The ZERO network has over 2,600 points of presence across 18 states in the country, with about a million enrolled customers, and is now on an exponential growth path, with firm mandates from various banks to expand its presence by 10 times within the current financial year itself. The system is used for cash deposits, cash withdrawal, transfer of money, disbursals of government benefits (pensions and wages under NREGA), disbursal of loans, collection of loan installments, collection of cash for third parties, insurance products and for payment of utility bills through the banking system.

ZMF has a BC settlement account with each of its 21 member banks, effectively making it a simple system for domestic payment and settlement of small value transactions across its multiple member banks, focused on low-value mass transaction at the bottom of the pyramid. It has created value and new opportunities with outstanding support from RBI, SBI and other banks to use innovative technologies and business processes in a vast market with large unfulfilled needs.

The solution enables:

- Robust, low cost enrollment of customers for multiple product categories—banking, telecom, insurance and government benefits based on common ID profile supported by biometrics.
- Cash and cashless collections, disbursals and transfers via the banking system.
- Implementation in a self-service OTA mode as well as OTC mode on consumer mobile phones, either as a secure PIN based application on SIM/J2ME, as well as an external tag with PIN verification using an over-the-counter Java mobile.
- Distribution and collection for micro-credit products for banks/other financial institutions.
- Distribution and collection for insurance products.
- Inward remittances (servicing the last mile).
- Distribution of products and services based on micro-credit offerings from Banks and other financial institutions.

In July 2007, SBI floated a 2-stage RFP for shortlisting and engaging technology service providers for its ambitious Financial Inclusion initiative. A Little World won the RFP, which effectively ended its pilot phase with SBI and established a clear framework to start commercial scale operations. The State Bank of India has since then expanded its financial inclusion portfolio using the SBI-Tiny product based on biometric authentication to 16 states. The platform was used to bring on board about 10,000 customers in the first 12 months (from July 2006 to June 2007). The landmark of 100,000 customers was reached in December 2007 and of 250,000 customers in March 2008.

After 18 months of real-world experience in diverse geographies across India, the platform has been re-engineered to prepare for larger scale and much more cost-effective operations. Today, the platform utilises extremely compact enrollment modules using a new generation mobile phone with a high-resolution camera and a small fingerprint scanner for biometric data capture. This makes it possible to carry out enrollments at a very fast pace with relatively less literate operators requiring minimal training. In fact, most of the enrollments are expertly carried out by 7th to 10th class pass women self-help group members. The operation of the transaction platform is even simpler.

Another recent landmark technology development on the same platform is the elimination of the need of a smart card for biometric authentication or account data management. New generation mobile phones with vast data storage and high end PKI based security allow the entire bank branch to be encapsulated within a mobile phone. Complete ID profiles of up to 50,000 customers, including their photographs, multiple fingerprints, multiple account types and transaction history of up to five years is stored in the secured memory area of the mobile phone.

A 9-digit serial number is issued to every customer, and is mapped to the customer's bank account. The customer just needs to bring this 9-digit number to an outlet in the village. No need of any smart card. This is an enormous saving for banks, of almost 80 per cent of the cost of infrastructure in a village, and is one of the many reasons for its popularity. The mobile uses bluetooth connectivity to link to a fingerprint scanner and printer for fulfilling a transaction. Transactions can be carried out both online and offline.

The system is completely self sufficient in communications, synchronising in auto or manual modes with the back-end through encrypted communications using the standard GPRS data network of multiple mobile operators. The platform has successfully demonstrated how to use technology to reduce costs, increase efficiency and make operations sustainable in the most difficult circumstances in all terrains. With the innovative use of mobile phones being the strong theme as well as the differentiator, the next stage of growth for the Zero platform is built around close cooperation with mobile telephony operators—to leverage their large geographic presence and huge customer base to increase penetration and to utilise the BC model to bring in a host of new service offerings to the hitherto unbanked mobile customers in villages, small towns and urban slums in the country.

Wadi Project

NABARD in 1995 launched a development initiative in parts of Gujarat and Maharashtra. Financed by a German government bank, this initiative came to be known as the Wadi project and was spread over 251 villages. This area of Gujarat where NABARD ran the programme has now been converted into a *wadi*, which means a small orchard.

The project area was largely a dryland and was inhabited by the tribals of that region for years. Most of the tribals in the area owned pockets of land ranging in size from one acre to five acres. Isolated from the mainstream development processes, the tribals had no access to education and were largely illiterate, depending upon certain old traditional ways of farming. They used to grow crops, such as millet, barley and ragi and made some income out of it. However with no access to fertilisers or pesticides or the science of cropping, their income from land was of a very uncertain kind, as a result of which many of them were forced to migrate from that area.

Following the release of the grant, NABARD decided to appoint an NGO to develop and carry out the programme and appointed BAIF Development Research Foundation as the development agency. The choice of BAIF was largely because of BAIF's impeccable record, knowledge and experience in carrying out development interventions.

The Wadi Programme has integrated cashew and mango cultivation and using that income the economic conditions of the families has improved. This also indirectly helped in improving the crop productivity of the land. BAIF's role was largely confined to providing technical know-how, and the programme implementation was done by the people themselves.

Water resources were developed by digging farm ponds, gully plugging and nala bunding for watering fruit plants during the initial 2-3 years. With a view to save time and cost on water conservation, temporary bunds were installed by stacking sandbags across the seasonal rivulets. Such nalas, which generally dry out in November, could retain water up to February-March months. The beneficiaries were able to carry headloads of water or pump it into their farm ponds and then water the fruit plants by hand. Pitcher watering was used to conserve water in areas of water shortage. In this method, an earthen pot with a minute hole plugged with a piece of cloth was placed near each plant, at about 15-30 cm below the ground level and filled with water. Water from the pitcher was released slowly into the soil around the plant. The pitcher was refilled with water once in 8-12 days. This helped in regular supply of moisture as in drip irrigation.

Looking back on the initial years of the project, BAIF essentially tried to educate the people about what was required for this type of agriculture.

They were given information on how to grow trees, tend towards them and the fertilisers to be used. It took almost two years to make them realise, that this could be done and that they need not migrate to other places in search of work.

A decade and more after the implementation of the Wadi Programme, things certainly have changed for the tribals in the region. "I migrated to Surat for work and used to get two or three thousand rupees. Food at home used to be served only once in a day and everyone did not get enough to eat," says Jaisingh Gavit of Lachakkadi village. "BAIF introduced me to horticulture, gave me training and I learnt from them. I planted mango and forestry trees. Starting from 1,000 grafts last year, and I made close to 10,000 grafts this year and sold 5,000 of them. From their sale, I have earned Rs. 100,000." His days of penury are now a thing of the past and he has built a permanent brick house for his family and is also the proud owner of a tractor and a motorcycle. His children now go to school regularly, and like he says, "there is enough food for all of us."

His sentiments are closely echoed by Ramal Bhai Litta of Dhamni village, who says that seven years ago there was only barren land and nothing would grow. After the introduction of the WADI Programme, says Ramal Bhai, "I was encouraged to grow mango and cashew." He today owns 20 mango trees, 40 cashew trees along with other forestry trees and has since last year started has started earning 10-15 thousand rupees a year.

Along with the Wadi Programme, BAIF also introduced other allied activities and under a capacity building programme, training programmes for the tribals were carried out. Training was imparted to over 6,600 tribals in making pot-drips, tailoring and vermicompost making. A number of other micro-enterprises were also put in place under the programme. Shanti Ben of Haidari village was given a loan of Rs. 5,000 to start a shop. "My family depends on earnings from this shop and I do not have to go anywhere else to work", says a contented Shanti Ben.

One of the initiatives under the Wadi Programme was the formation of self help groups. Most of the women earlier had to work as labour on somebody else's farms. Many times they were cheated by the landlords and did not getting sufficient remuneration for the work that they were doing. BAIF encouraged the women to form SHGs and to start developing a savings habit. Today, over 648 SHGs are operating in the project area and using their savings have started several income generating activities.

Gauri Ben Raghubhai of Dhamni village is one such member of a SHG group. She along with four other women started making vermicompost, most of which was used in their own fields. The remaining vermicompost was then sold in the market. "We also sell the worms to others", informs Gauri Ben, "and this gives all of us sufficient incomes." Valki Ben of Dhaku village too used to work as a labourer to collect bamboo from the jungle from which she would earn Rs. 20-25 a day. "We were encouraged to form a group of five women and were given training by BAIF to make pot-drips that are used in the plantations. By selling these I earn about Rs. 70 a day", says Valki Ben, as her SHG partners nod their heads in acknowledgement.

These groups could play a significant role in motivating all the members to take active part and assist each other whenever needed. Hence, creation of awareness, transfer of technologies and programme monitoring could be undertaken very effectively. These groups also took the responsibility of procuring necessary inputs from the market and distributing among the members. As these activities were linked with micro-financing, all the participating families could procure the inputs well in time and the repayment was also effective.

In this process of capacity building, many common people, including illiterate women, emerged as community leaders and contested in the elections of Panchayati Raj Institutions, cooperative societies and took initiative in community development. They established linkages with various financial institutions and banks to meet their credit needs. These organisations are playing a vital role in sustaining the programme benefits and progress, even after the end of financial support from the donor agencies.

Another resounding success was the formation of the Women's Milk Cooperative. Started as a SHG, its members contributed Rs. 10 each month for a year and used that money for lending at 5 per cent interest. They then later bought calves for the members and formed a milk cooperative. Today the cooperative is a big success story and basking in its glow is an ecstatic member Vanita Ben Patel who tells us that each member earns about Rs. 4,000-5,000 each month from the sale of milk.

According to NABARD, "the women have got a lot of impetus out of their experience with SHGs and today were not just content with production and wanted to look beyond that into starting processing of various products." Production of mango pulp and pickles has already started providing them forward market linkages and the SHGs are looking at other activities too. Processing has also opened up new avenues for jobs and employs a large number of women and men. Malati Ben of Lachakkadi village, who works in one of the processing units belongs to a poor family and had to drop from school since her father could not afford the cost of putting her through school. A confident Malati today says, "By working here, I will save money and resume my studies later."

The Rs. 1.30 billion programme touches the lives of over 25,000 families in Gujarat and Maharashtra. Before the project, most of the tribals lived in *kuccha* houses. The implementation of the Wadi Programme has ushered in a change in the lives of the people. They are economically sound, have built *pucca* houses and their children go to school regularly. The project has delivered and can be summed up through the eyes of the beneficiaries. The tribals today look to the future with confidence and the planting of each tree is like planting a new ray of hope for them and their families.

Annexures

Poverty

Microfinance Community

Solution Exchange for the Microfinance Community Consolidated Reply

Query: Speeding Financial Inclusion through a Common Strategy - Experiences; Advice

Compiled by Navin Anand, Resource Person and Monika Khanna, Research Associate
Issue Date: 30 June 2009

From Sameer Kochhar, Skoch Development Foundation, Gurgaon
Posted 5 June 2009

Past several years have seen the words 'financial inclusion' and 'inclusive growth' becoming a part of the common man's glossary as well as a factor in the development agenda, cutting across the whole spectrum. In the same period, quite a bit of experimentation has happened across the country and multiple stakeholders have tried to contribute in their own ways.

An attempt to make a problem tree of financial inclusion projects and programmes will help us to visualize the gamut of factors of exclusion existing in different socio-economic contexts of India. This makes the task of financial inclusion more complex and therefore a systemic approach to address the problem is required. The learning from various experiments undertaken in past few years provides us knowledge about the factors of success as well as failures. At this juncture, it is important to take a consolidated view of all the learning so as to fill in the gaps and suggest a common path to address the issue of financial inclusion.

In order to suggest a common strategy, we have undertaken a nation wide multi-stakeholder study entitled **"Speeding Financial Inclusion - Technology, Business and Regulatory Scan."** The study entails - one on one interviews, field visits as well as research meetings of practitioners and domain experts.

We believe that the study would not be complete without taking note of and learning from the community input, we find it prudent to get the experiences and views of the members and domain experts on the following:

- To what extent you find Banking Correspondents (BCs) model appropriate for financial inclusion in context of the viability of banks, benefits to BCs and supply of services to the clients. What do you suggest to strengthen the BC model?
- What changes are required in the availability/norms for microfinance products and services (micro-credit, savings, micro-insurance, micro-pensions and micro-investment) so as to fast track the process of financial inclusion?
- What do you think are appropriate uses for the Financial Inclusion Fund (FIF) and the Financial Inclusion Technology Fund (FITF)?

The inputs of the members will be useful in formulating a common strategy for financial inclusion. The study is expected to be presented during our **summit** focused on Inclusive Growth at Mumbai on 16 - 17 July 2009.

Responses were received, with thanks, from

1. **Jaya Patel, World Food Programme, Uttarkashi, Uttarakhand**
2. **Akhil K. Srivastava, Antardrishti, Agra, Uttar Pradesh**
3. **Hemalatha Ramasubramanian, Rai Business School, New Delhi**
4. **Vivek Kaul, New Delhi**
5. **Atul Rawat, DMV Business and Market Research Private Limited, Hyderabad**
6. **N. Jeyaseelan, Helping Hand Micro Finance and Services, Kancheepuram, Tamil Nadu**
7. **T. Balasubramanian, Mudhal Inclusive Growth Foundation, Chennai**
8. **Toms K. Thomas, Mutual Assistance Resource Group (MARG), Trihur, Kerala**
9. **Navin Anand, United Nations Development Programme, New Delhi**
10. **Indu Chandra Ram, AFC Consultants International, Germany**
11. **Santanu Sengupta, Micro Money Management Enterprise (MMME), Kolkata**
12. **D B S Prasad, Andhra Pradesh State Cooperative Bank, Hyderabad**
13. **Subhash Wadhwa, Independent Consultant, Mumbai**
14. **Sameer Kochhar, Skoch Development Foundation, Gurgaon**

Further contributions are welcome!

Summary of Responses
Comparative Experiences
Related Resources
Responses in Full

Summary of Responses

Delivering financial services at an affordable cost to the various sections of the society has been prime focus of various microfinance institutions, regulators and Government. Over the years many steps have been undertaken to fast track the process however a lot has to be done. Members identified a dire need to formulate a common strategy whereby the institutions shall play a complementary role to each other.

Responding to the query, members suggested analyzing various environments (micro environment, intermediary and macro) in which the financial services are provided to the poor. Moreover, for speeding up the financial inclusion process addressing all the three environments is necessary as they are interdependent and interlinked to each other.

Suggestions for speeding up the Financial Inclusion process

- Clear segmentation of the population that is financially excluded and thereby formulating a strategy and plan for inclusion
- Using the existing networks - Post Offices, well functioning Panchayats, Primary Agriculture Cooperatives Societies (PACS), District Cooperative Banks, Money Lenders
- Customizing the products as per the geographic requirements and providing the incentives to the organizations/institutions working in the remote and difficult areas

- Extensive use of technology – mobile phone banking, kiosks providing virtual banking services
- Capacity building of the human resource engaged in the process of providing the financial services

Suggesting a way to fast track the financial inclusion process, members shared that instead of opening new branches in remote areas, Business Correspondents can easily extend the financial services at an affordable rate. Members shared that PACS, Urban cooperative banks, Salary Earners Thrift and Credit Cooperatives, post offices, insurance agents, small retail shop owners could be some of the possible business correspondents. Also the people with disabilities could avail livelihood opportunity by becoming the business correspondents.

Members also shared good experiments of existing network of financial service delivery institutions that can suitably adopt themselves as Business Correspondents. India Post has been offered by Uttaranchal Gramin Bank to function as a BC. Many PACS are also functioning as mini banks with substantial amount of savings with them, these PACS can be utilized for routing financial services. Referring to the successful pilots in urban areas, members mentioned the work of Cuttak Urban Cooperative Bank, Orissa where the agents are used for daily collection of deposits and recovery and can successfully take up the role of a BC. Similarly the salary earners thrift and credit cooperatives having surplus money available with them can effectively function as a business correspondent.

Suggestions for strengthening the Business Correspondent Model

Realizing the importance of Business Correspondents in the overall financial inclusion process, members acknowledge the revised guidelines introduced by the Reserve Bank of India (RBI), whereby the maximum distance for BC is extended from 15 to 30 kilometers. Members opined that BC model is a good route to achieve the financial inclusion process. However, members also shared their concern towards the financial literacy of the business correspondent as one of the major issue that needs to be addressed. Some of the recommendations to strengthen the business correspondent model suggested by the members are as follows:

- Commission structure offered by the banks to the business correspondents needs to be revised so that it could cover the operational cost on a sustainable manner
- Initial security deposit asked by the banks from the BCs could be covered under the credit guarantee fund
- Linkages of financial literacy and credit counseling centers with the BCs could fast track the financial inclusion. BCs could function as service provider as well as counselor for providing customized financial services
- For increasing the participation of disadvantaged sections of society, RBI has to simplify the norms and facilitate more people to participate as BCs

Referring to the financial inclusion fund and financial inclusion technology fund members shared that these funds can fill the resource gap and can easily fast track the financial inclusion. However members shared that as per the existing policy the MFIs/NGO-MFIs cannot submit the proposal directly to the NABARD for utilizing the FIF and FITF funds. The proposal has to be routed through banks and the participating agency is entrusted with 25 percent grant and has to bear 75 percent on their own, members shared that if the participating agency could directly submit the proposal, a lot of time in taking up innovative project can be saved. Some of the other suggestions for properly utilizing the FIF and FITF funds by members were:

- Providing common infrastructure – mobile ATMs, mobile phones, facilitating electronic money transfers
- Subsidizing the point of sale devices used by the BCs for transfer of money

- Channelizing more money for enhancing linkages of MFIs with banks for reaching the disadvantage sections of the society
- Setting up Financial Literary and Counseling Centers
- Raising the current grant proportions from existing 25 percent will encourage creativity of the resource starved agencies

Finally members shared that for achieving the financial inclusion agenda, all the organizations engaged in the process of providing financial services need to work collaboratively. There is already a network of many institutions that had existed from a long time and had served masses in the underserved areas. There is a need to build the capacities of the existing networks, with a little effort and optimally using the technology we can achieve financial inclusion at a faster and sustainable manner.

Comparative Experiences

Uttarakhand

India Post tied up with Uttaranchal Gramin Bank *(from Vivek Kaul, New Delhi)*
India Post had tied up with Uttaranchal Gramin Bank to function as a Business Correspondent on behalf of bank. The partnership aimed towards disbursing bank loan, collection of the repayment installments through saving account. This has helped the bank to extend the financial services in the remote areas using the existing network of India Post. Rural population would be able to get the financial services at their doorstep through a network of 2500 post office branches

From Monika Khanna, Research Associate

Tamil Nadu

Information Kiosks Gives Rural Communities Access to Services through Internet
Rural Access to services through Internet (RASI), focused on setting up internet-based information Kiosk in every panchayat through SHGs. The SHGs were assisted through subsidy-cum-credit linked finance under SGSY to set up the kiosk. Members were also trained on how to operate the kiosk. The main income for the SHG members managing the kiosks was through providing access to essential needs and by providing accurate and timely information. It was implemented in 10 districts during 2003 - 2004. Read more

Punjab

India Post to function as Business Correspondent for a Bank
State Bank of India has entered into an alliance with India Post to provide banking facilities to the people in rural areas of Punjab. Initially, India Post will only act as a business facilitator and will mobilize business for the bank. Subsequently, the post offices will act as business correspondents and carry out the transactions through Point of Sales (POS) machines installed at the link post offices. Read more

---

Related Resources

Recommended Documentation

Financial Inclusion by Extension of Banking Services *(from Akhil K. Srivastava, Antardrishti, Agra, Uttar Pradesh)*

Circular; Reserve Bank of India; January 25, 2006
http://rbidocs.rbi.org.in/rdocs/Notification/PDFs/68417.pdf (PDF; Size: 66 KB)

Circular introducing the Banking Correspondent and Facilitators model to ensure greater financial inclusion and increase the outreach of the banking sector

Financial Inclusion by Extension of Banking Services – Use of Business Facilitators (BFs) and Business Correspondents (BCs) (*from Jaya Patel, World Food Programme, Uttarkashi, Uttarakhand)*
Circular; Reserve Bank Of India; 24 April 2009
Available at http://www.rbi.org.in/scripts/BS_CircularIndexDisplay.aspx?Id=4950 (PDF Size: 55.9 KB)

Shares the increase in maximum distance criteria for the operation of a Business Correspondent for rural, semi-urban and urban areas from the existing 15 kms to 30 kms

From Navin Anand, United Nations Development Programme, New Delhi

Financial Literacy and Credit Counseling Centers (FLCCs) - Model Scheme
Circular; Reserve Bank of India; 4 February 2009
Available at http://rbidocs.rbi.org.in/rdocs/notification/PDFs/FLCCCIR1.pdf (PDF; Size: 46.4 KB)

Shares the model scheme of opening counselling centres, either individually or with pooled resources, for credit and technological counselling

Task Force on Revival of Cooperative Credit Structure (Dr. Vaidyanathan Committee Report)
Report; Reserve Bank of India; 11 January 2005
Available at http://www.rbi.org.in/scripts/PublicationReportDetails.aspx?FromDate=01/11/2005&SECID=21&SUBSECID=0

Report deals with the issue of reviving and revitalizing the rural cooperative credit structure (CCS) including cooperative banks and PACS

From Monika Khanna, Research Associate

Kiosks Run by the SHGs
Guidelines; Rural Development and Panchayti Raj Department, Government of Tamil Nadu; September 2003
Available at http://priasoft1.tn.nic.in/rdwebsite/Central_Schemes/linkfiles/go_rd_205_03_pg177.pdf (PDF Size: 51 KB)

Shares the guidelines by SGSY to set up Internet based information Kiosk in every panchayat through self help groups

SBI - India Post Tie-up to Provide Banking Facilities in Rural Punjab
Article; The Financial Express; 15 July 2008
Available at http://www.financialexpress.com/news/SBIIndia-Post-tieup-to-provide-banking-facilities-in-rural-Punjab/335652/

India Post to function as a Business Correspondent of State Bank of India for providing banking facilities to the people in rural areas

Recommended Organizations and Programmes

Reserve Bank of India (RBI), Mumbai *(from Jaya Patel, World Food Programme, Uttarkashi, Uttarakhand)*

Rural Planning and Credit Department, Central Office Building, 13th Floor, Mumbai 400 001; Tel.: 91-22- 22610261; Fax: 91-22- 22658276;
http://www.rbi.org.in/scripts/AboutUsDisplay.aspx?pg=Depts.htm#RPCD

Rural Planning and Credit Department of RBI formulates policies relating to rural credit and monitors timely and adequate flow of credit

From Akhil K. Srivastava, Antardrishti, Agra, Uttar Pradesh

National Handicapped Finance and Development Corporation (NHFDC), Faridabad
Red Cross Bhawan, Sector-12, Faridabad 121007 Haryana; Tel: 91-129-2287512, 91-129-2287513; Fax: 91-129-2284371; nhfdc@nda.vsnl.net.in;
http://www.nhfdc.org/site/micro_sca.aspx

Provides loans for self-employment and other economic ventures to the people with a disability

National Bank for Agriculture and Rural Development (NABARD), Mumbai
Plot No. C-24, "G" Block, Bandra-Kurla Complex, P. B. No 8121, Bandra (E), Mumbai 400051; Tel.: 91-22-2653 9244; Fax: 91-22-2652-8141; nabmcid@vsnl.com;
http://www.nabard.org/roles/microfinance/index.htm

Apex institution providing loan funds for microfinance services in the form of revolving fund assistance to NGO-MFIs, SHG Federations and NGOs to lend to SHGs

Swarna Jayanti Gram Swarozgar Yojana (SGSY), New Delhi
Krishi Bhawan, New Delhi 110001; Tel: 91-11-23782373/27; Fax: 91-11-23385876;
http://www.rural.nic.in

Poverty alleviation programme that provides micro-credit and group insurance services to the poor through SHGs.

State Bank of India, Mumbai *(from Vivek Kaul, New Delhi)*
Tulsini Chamber, 1st Floor, West Wing, 212, Free Press Journal Marg, Nariman Point, Mumbai 400021 Maharashtra; Tel: 91-22-22820427; Fax: 91-22-22820411; crpd@sbi.co.in;
http://www.statebankofindia.com/viewsection.jsp?lang=0&id=0,8,67

Nationalized public sector bank tied up with Postal Department for piloting business facilitator and business correspondent model

From Navin Anand, United nations Development Programme, New Delhi

Bandhan, Kolkata
EC-76, Sector-1, Salt Lake City, Kolkata 700064 West Bengal; Tel: 91-33–23346751; Fax: 91-33-2334613; info@bandhanmf.com; http://www.bandhanmf.com/micro_loan.html

One of the largest MFIs in eastern India, has been entrusted by CGAP to pilot ultra poor programme in West Bengal

SKS , Andhra Pradesh
Maruti Mansion, Municipal No.2-3-578/1, Kachi Colony, Nallagutta, Minister Road, Secunderabad 500003 Andhra Pradesh; Tel: 91-40-44526000; Fax: 91-40-44526001; info@sksindia.com;
http://www.sksindia.com/sksultrapoor.htm

Microfinance institution running ultra poor programme that aims to meets the needs of ultra poor on multiple levels: economic, health and social

Cuttack Urban Cooperative Bank, Orissa
Tinikonia Bagicha, Buxi Bazar, Cuttack 753001 Orissa; Tel: 91-671-2425013; Fax: 91-671-2425014; mail ho@urbanco-opbankctc.com; http://www.urbanco-opbankctc.com/deposit-schemes/

Cooperative bank aims to provide financial assistance to the urban poor for their upliftment through microfinance

Sewa Bank, Ahmadabad
109, Sakar-II, Opp. Town Hall, Ellisbridge, Ahmedabad 380006 Gujarat; Tel: 91-79-26576054; Fax: 91-79-26581597; mail@sewabank.com; http://www.sewabank.com/savings-general.htm

Aims at providing an integrated set of banking services to its women clients and it was first cooperative to start mobile banking in India

Trickle Up, United States of America
104 W 27th Street, 12th Floor, New York 10001-6210; Tel: 212-255-9980; Fax: 212-255-9974; daynellew@trickleup.org; http://www.trickleup.org/ourwork/asia program.html

Livelihood development organization pioneering a new project in India with funding and support from CGAP to provide business/vocational training and seed capital grants

Zero Mass Foundation (ZMF), Mumbai *(from Monika Khanna, Research Associate)*
10-11, Shubhada B-Wing, Sir Pochkhanwala Road, Worli, Mumbai 400025 Maharashtra; Tel: 91-22-66173888; Fax: 91-22-66173999; ceo@alittleworld.com; http://www.alittleworld.com/htmls/zmf.html

Works as a Business Correspondent (BC) of multiple banks for extending banking services in villages

Related Consolidated Replies

Microfinance through Post Offices for Financial Inclusion, from P. Das, National Bank for Agriculture and Rural Development, Uttarakhand (Experiences; Advice). Microfinance Community, Solution Exchange - India,
Issued 5 March 2009. Available at http://www.solutionexchange-un.net.in/mf/cr/cr-se-mf-15120801.pdf (PDF; Size: 221 KB)

Seeks experiences on successful experiments of micro financing through post offices and suggestions on innovative use of the NABARD's financial inclusion funds

Financial Inclusion in the North Eastern Region, from T. Keyzom Ngodup, Consultant, Mumbai (Advice; Referrals). Microfinance Community, Solution Exchange - India,
Issued 8 June 2009. Available at http://www.solutionexchange-un.net.in/mf/cr/cr-se-mf-08060901.pdf (PDF; Size: 173 KB)

Seeks referrals of programmes/projects for financial inclusion in NER and explores strategies for collaborations and convergence with different stakeholders in NER

Responses in Full

Jaya Patel, World Food Programme, Uttarkashi, Uttarakhand

Mr. Sameer has raised relevant questions on financial inclusion. In the mountain areas like Uttarakhand, focused interventions are required for financial inclusion. Some of the specific issues of the hilly region are:

- Low density of population in the districts of hilly region such as Chamoli, Almora, Nainital, Pithoragarh, Rudraprayag, Uttarkashi, Tehri Garhwal, Pauri Garhwal

- Bank branches are located more than 30 km away from the villages in many districts
- Cultivable land holdings are small in size and therefore the loan requirements for agriculture is low
- Farmers need loan for infrastructure facilities such as poly-houses, mini-warehouses and sheds for dairy animals
- Risk factors in hills are high and crop insurance facilities are not need based
- Health insurance services are different in nature – people need support for travel and health insurance services are needed for catering day to health problems rather than hospitalization. Normally, health insurance schemes do not cover all these problems
- Due to the problem of marketing of farm and non farm produce, people require short term but timely credit facilities

Business Correspondent/Business Facilitator model introduced by Reserve Bank of India (RBI) is a good initiative for financial inclusion. Moreover, we welcome the revised circular of RBI in which the maximum distance criteria for BC is revised from 15 km to 30 km. The broadening of eligibility criteria for Business correspondents will be beneficial for mountain states as ex-servicemen from armed forces can undertake this activity very well.

In mountain regions, this single scheme with the inputs of technology can change the situation. Since mountain region has specific requirements, so Government and NABARD have to customize the schemes for mountain and remote areas by giving special incentives and provisions to the banks, MFIs and clients. The industrial policy of Uttarakhand has a provision of rebate in the interest for the remote areas. The entrepreneur has to apply for getting the interest rebate after availing and paying the normal interest rates. Due to procedural hassles, very few entrepreneurs apply for the rebate. Hence, the rebate needs to be direct and inbuilt in the scheme.

In mountain region we need innovative microfinance products and services such as:

- Medium term credit for farm infrastructure
- Micro insurance services customized to the needs of the mountain people such as insurance for snake bite cases, micro health insurance packages for acute health problems etc.
- Remittance services through mobile phone banking services

Financial Inclusion Fund (FIF) and the Financial Inclusion Technology Fund (FITF) could be used for providing common infrastructure for financial inclusion like mobile ATMs, mobile phones and machines/tools for transfer of money to Business Correspondents at reduced rates.

Akhil K. Srivastava, Antardrishti, Agra, Uttar Pradesh

Antardrishti is Agra based social development organization and it is committed to the cause of blind people in our society. Since we are working with visually impaired, I would to like to focus my response on the issue of financial inclusion for People with Disabilities (PwDs). Financial inclusion for PwDs, especially with visually impaired is very difficult because majority of the programmes focus on SHG model and it is difficult to form a group of disabled people in a village or in a hamlet of any urban locality. There are few initiatives focusing on individual model. Three years back, I personally tried to link visually impaired people in Agra with National Handicapped Finance and Development Corporation (NHFDC). Due to lack of confidence, proper training and almost no link with market, the initiatives were withdrawn.

Apart from NHFDC, SHG bank linkage programme of NABARD and SGSY programme of rural development department are two national level initiatives expected to cover PwDs. The SGSY programme gives privilege to PwDs by including 5-10 members in a SHG. The subsidy component for the PwDs under this scheme is also higher than general category people. Based on my observations in rural areas, I can say that these two programmes could cover a limited number of PwDs. All this shows that we need an innovative mechanism to reach these people with options of microfinance products and services suited to their needs. The NGOs working with people with disabilities will be motivated to provide microfinance services if they get some operational grant from the Government to develop a proper system.

The Business Correspondent (BC)/Business Facilitator (BF) model, (http://rbidocs.rbi.org.in/rdocs/Notification/PDFs/68417.pdf) could be a panacea for the problems of PwDs, as most of these people are scattered, staying in different areas and need handholding support. The RBI has relaxed the conditions for becoming Business Correspondents, but still there is a scope for expansion. Why not a grocery shop owner functions as a Business Correspondent? Ms. Jaya Patel has rightly mentioned about the constraints of mountain and remote areas. In some of the remote villages, a small grocery shop is the only common place visited by the poor. If the poor are already taking loans from these grocery shop owners then why not make it formal and link them with banks. In this way, banks will also be able to monitor the activities of these informal financers and can get economic information about the people.

Hemalatha Ramasubramanian, Rai Business School, New Delhi

I am closely following the discussions going on in this forum. I would like to add a few points.

It is really a good idea to connect the retail grocery shops. The other place frequently visited by the people is the hospital or PHC where there can be links for insurance. Financial inclusion will need a backing of insurance for cattle, life and property. Only then we can imagine any improvement in the life of the poor. Not only blind, but all the differently able people need assistance as the PwDs are marginalized in villages. There is a need for policy interventions in all the remotest villages of northeast, hilly areas of Himachal, Uttarakhand etc.

Vivek Kaul, New Delhi

I have worked as Chief Postmaster General, Uttarakhand and had a close watch on the "Business Correspondent (BC) model". The State Bank of India has already offered India Post to function as a BC and it is at a pilot stage.

Business Correspondence Model at individual/NGO level has its own limitations. Some of these are –

- Lack of credibility with the rural populace on the individual business correspondent for investing money through him
- The rural population is also not very comfortable with high technology procedures like biometric cards, for their ignorance and lack of confidence in such technologies
- The business correspondent may not find the model viable to be operated in a village. The model should be able to create sufficient and long run income for the BC to remain engaged in this business

Post Office, on the other hand, has a definite edge as an institution that can operate as a successful business correspondent. I would like to share a draft that covers potential of Post Office as a successful agent for financial inclusion in Indian rural scenario. To read the document, please visit: www.solutionexchange-un.net.in/mf/cr/res05060901.doc (Size: 59 KB)

If members are convinced, this model could be further elaborated upon. Queries are welcome from the group.

Atul Rawat, DMV Business and Market Research Private Limited, Hyderabad

Changes which are required in the availability for microfinance products and services are:

- Increase the role of technology in microfinance (MIS, cash handling, data processing)
- Creation of new MFIs (Venture Capital)
- Check and control fraud
- Encouraging telecom and internet service providing companies to work in rural areas

The Financial Inclusion Fund (FIF) should be used for the upliftment of the lower income group and people living below poverty line. This fund can do wonder, if it is used wisely. The most feasible would be to make a small microfinance community or insurance coverage for covering a significant population. The making of local supervisory body would enhance the trust and confidence of the locals in the process. The linkage of MFIs with banks could be used to reach the underprivileged group.

On the other hand, Financial Inclusion Technology Fund, which is a part of FIF, has to be used for setting up of financial literacy centers, launching a financial literacy campaign or following industry standards for applying industry standard.

For further details, please refer these links-

http://www.iibf.org.in/portal/documents/fininclusion_jindal.ppt#317,12,Funds (Size: 299 KB)

http://www.inafiindia.in/Brochure%20-%20MF%20&%20FI%20Regional%20Conference%20&%20Forum.pdf (Size: 521 KB)

N. Jeyaseelan, Helping Hand Micro Finance and Services, Kancheepuram, Tamil Nadu

Financial inclusion is a thrust area, which has the potential to ensure the inclusive growth and equitable distribution of credit access to the underserved and unserved segments of the society.

While as an NGO we wanted to make use of the Financial Inclusion Technology Fund (FITF), to facilitate financial inclusion through our Village Knowledge Kiosks (Citizen Centers). We faced a problem in the existing policy that the proposal has to be submitted to NABARD through a bank and the grant eligible is only 25 percent and the participating agency should bear 75 percent.

Using the technology will expedite the financial inclusion. Also, the following changes will speed up the financial inclusion-

- NGO should be made as an eligible agency to submit the proposals directly under the FITF, as the NGO will be taking up innovative need based projects for financial inclusion
- The eligible grant portion should be raised to 75 percent for big NGOs/MFIs and for small NGOs/MFIs, it should be 90 percent and the margin from the promoting agency should be brought down so as to ensure that the creativity of an agency should not be limited because of resource constraints. Innovations should be encouraged with lot of in built flexibilities
- Banking Correspondent (BC) model is a good route to achieve financial inclusion. But, the existing commission structure offered by banks is not viable to cover the cost of operations on a sustainable basis. RBI may allow BC to charge a reasonable fee from the clients in a transparent way

- Banks ask security deposits from BCs and really committed NGOs without adequate financial resources are not able to provide the security deposit to the banks. Hence, the guarantee cover available under the credit guarantee fund trust shall be extended to cover BCs also
- Most of the banks are satisfied with just opening of the "No frills account " and announce that 100 percent financial inclusion is achieved. They should go one step further and make available the needed financial services i.e. credit, remittance or insurance as the case may be to the underserved/unserved segments, so that they will also be mainstreamed from their marginalized position.

The above measures will go a long way in speeding up the financial inclusion.

T. Balasubramanian, Mudhal Inclusive Growth Foundation, Chennai

One should understand the need and the possible impact of financial inclusion before going in to the real subject.

There are two types of people who have to be financially included. Firstly, one who don not have access to any financial services either directly or indirectly through private money lenders. Secondly, those people who are presently exploited by the private money lenders.

The first categories of people are underutilized of the potentials, because they do not have finance to either enhance the capabilities or to better utilize their existing resources. I can explain some typical cases however I leave it to the visualizations of the readers to imagine the situation, were the poor is suffering because of the non availability of the financial services.

The second categories of people are always kept into the debt trap. Most of their hard earned money is exhausted in the form of paying exorbitant amount in the form of interest.

If we could be able to make the financial services available at minimum cost and financial inclusion in reality, then the dreams of our beloved Mahatmaji and Vinobhaji will become a reality and parity will be created among the people. Financial inclusion will create alternative source of competitiveness from the poor. There is possibility of getting cost effective, high quality output at a competitive price. Financial inclusion can make this possible, which in turn will result in speeding up the economic wheel.

Every one will agree that through establishing physical banks in all places may be the right solution for financial inclusion. But for speeding up the process, the only solution is using technology. Mobile banking, virtual money, kiosks providing virtual banking services are the tested solutions readily available for speedy financial inclusion. The financial services which are available to certain section of poor, reaches them at a very huge cost except the no frill bank accounts. The cost increases because of the layers in the supply chain. There are several layers it has to cross before reaching the actual client. We should use technology to cut down layers and minimize the operating cost to enable the real financial inclusion.

In Tamil Nadu, the Government is providing televisions and gas stoves to the poor, similar schemes may be available in most of the states. The political leaders can think of giving a mobile phone with life time validity and a monthly free talk time for Rs. 25. This can revolutionize the speed of financial inclusion. Providing mobile phone for free with minimum services is surely possible. Government jointly with BSNL and MTNL could come out with a product which is cheaper than Rs. 1000. Using mobile phones and reaching the unreached is surely possible now, mobile technology is already revolutionizing in countries like Philippines, Indonesia in providing financial services. By providing one mobile phone to a poor, we can come out with several solutions and surely it will speed up the financial inclusion if we make appropriate policy interventions to enable these mobile technology in all financial transactions and allowing the electronic money transfer between mobiles.

The Government has to create depository for electronic money, such us National Securities Depository Limited (NSDL) and Central Depository Services (India) Limited (CDSL) as in the case of electronic share transfers. Banks and mobile operators have to act as participants and the mobile users can be allowed to use their mobile as their electronic wallet. By creating electronic money we can speed up the financial inclusion using mobile.

The Banking Correspondent model will surely fuel the reach of the financial inclusion. RBI has to simplify the norms and facilitate more people to participate as banking correspondents.

Only when we start using technology, we can think of improving the norms of microfinance product. There is huge scope of improvement in microfinance product. A healthy competition will also facilitate creation of more microfinance products.

I understand that the financial inclusion fund and the financial inclusion technology fund are not utilized properly. It should be in the hands of the people who are positive about the financial inclusion and about the importance of technology intervention in enabling financial inclusion. Without positive outlook for future, it may not be possible to take decisions to support the right concepts/projects. I am very sure there are several projects which deserve support but are hesitant to approach these funds for obvious reasons.

Toms K. Thomas, Mutual Assistance Resource Group (MARG), Trihur, Kerala

The issue pointed by Sameer needs further discussion and it is very important in the context of the present financial crisis across the globe. I should first of all suggest that financial inclusion is not same as open credit provision. Financial inclusion requires things beyond credit. It is a mechanism to ensure better economic participation than just triggering spending one component of financial inclusion. The financial openness and risk taking ability created within the microfinance clients are two very important requirements to ensure financial inclusion, through credit could ensure economic growth.

I am not very much optimistic at the present business correspondence model rather it could be improved through further innovation by integrating other issues of financial inclusion along with the credit. The financial literacy issue of the business correspondents also is a big issue and it needs to be addressed.

I do like the word in the query - common strategy. However, I fear if a common strategy is possible since often MFIs lack orientation towards this and function very similar to commercial banks. Economic reactivation through microfinance requires a careful analysis of the client profile of the organizations before economic intervention. I do agree that a common strategy or a joint effort could result in improving the outcomes of the financial inclusion efforts and can minimize risks.

Most of the MFIs in fact are not very serious in working in partnership because of the inbuilt fear of them about their business. My pasty experience with a few MFIs suggest that MFIs needs to come out of the fear of financial risking because of emergence of new competitors or similar organizations, rather they should be promoters of joint interventions which definitely could better the outreach along with reducing the financial risk.

Financial Inclusion Fund is a good idea but there is a need of thinking about various associated issues like credit modalities, client category, MFI willingness etc before getting into it. Yes, I strongly agree that a joint intervention is the need of the hour. I should appreciate the changes that are happening with in the formal financial sector towards common strategies. But unfortunately most of the MFIs still have the inward orientation towards this.

Navin Anand, United Nations Development Programme, New Delhi

The issue of financial inclusion can be seen more systematically by classifying the whole system of providing financial services to poor into three environments –

- **Micro Environment** : (Retail formal and informal financial institutions such as SHGs, Federations, Thrift and Credit Cooperatives, Primary Agriculture Cooperative Societies/Groups and individual suppliers including individual Business Correspondents (BCs)/ Facilitators (BFs) etc.)
- **Intermediary Environment** : (Wholesale/Semi-Wholesale financial institutions, National Banks, Apex Institutions of Ministries undertaking microfinance services, MFIs working at the State level or in Multi states, microfinance projects and programmes)
- **Macro Environment:** (Policy and Regulatory Bodies like IRDA, RBI, Government of India/State Governments, credit bureaus, donors, international agencies and platforms supporting networks and collaborations, money transfer and payment systems, training and research institutions, knowledge management networks etc. The organizations and departments in the external environment are not directly involved in the value chains of the microfinance but influence and support the internal environment of financial inclusion system)

For speeding up financial inclusion agenda, addressing all the three environments is necessary as these environments are linked with each other and are interdependent.

Suggestions for speeding up Financial Inclusion

Clear Segmentation of the Target Groups – It is important to have a fine segmentation of the people who are excluded socially and financially. One will find that majority of the socially excluded people are also financially excluded. The classification of the target group could be in following different ways-

- Rural, Semi-urban and Urban poor
- Scheduled Caste, Scheduled Tribes, Backward people, physically and mentally challenged people including visually impaired, poor widows, transient laborers and poor people from minority class.
- People living in mountain and remote areas (including those living in border areas where Microfinance institutions and bank branch network is low)
- Poor senior citizens, daily/monthly wage earners in urban areas migrated from different states who do not have any identity proof required by the banks and formal financing agencies)

The segmentation of different categories of people will help in formulating a different strategy and plan for inclusion.

Introduction of Ultra Poor and Target Group Specific Projects – There are many programmes and projects of Government, banks and NGOs/MFIs that are covering poor, however for financial inclusion there is a need for more focused ultra poor projects. The CGAP and Ford Foundation's initiative of funding pilots in five sites for ultra poor programme is a good example of including ultra poor. Bandhan and Trickle Up in West Bengal and SKS in Andhra Pradesh have successfully taken up the pilots.

Besides ultra poor, as mentioned above, there are other categories/segment of people who are socially excluded and vulnerable. There is a need for having specific programmes for different target groups. The Government programmes like SGSY (Swarna Jayanti Gram Swarojgar Yojana), PMRY (Prime Minister Rojgar Yojana) and other such initiatives do focus poor but these programmes could be strengthened by adopting multiple strategies for covering different subsets of people.

Using existing networks more creatively

The networks of **Primary Agriculture Cooperative Societies (PACS),** Post Offices and Panchayats have been the biggest networks in the country, serving rural masses.

Using PACS and Cooperative Network

There have been good experiments of using PACS as Self Help Promotion Institutions to include the poor through SHGs. The Bidar District Cooperative Bank (DCCB) in Karnataka and many other DCCBs in West Bengal and other states have undertaken the financial inclusion initiative. The PACS having mini banks are able to function more effectively as financial intermediaries for poor. Some of the mini banks in Kerala, Western districts of UP and Nainital district of Uttarakhand are having deposits of even more than Rs. 10 millions. After implementation of Vaidyanathan Committee's recommendations, these PACS will be having more autonomy and could act as **good Business Correspondents**. In Urban areas, thrift and credit societies formed through SHGs or individuals could be tested for financial inclusion. The **Cuttack Urban Cooperative Bank, Orissa** has used agents for daily collection of deposits and recovery in last few years. They can immediately adopt BC/BF model to upscale their business. The SEWA Bank, Ahmedabad is also an example of an Urban Cooperative Bank working for financial inclusion. They were the first to start Mobile Banking in India for serving rural clients.

There are number of **Salary Earners Thrift and Credit Cooperatives** which are in profits and having surplus money to lend. The SHGs of ultra poor and excluded people can be linked with these cooperatives for financial inclusion. In this arrangement the provision of nominal membership can be used by these cooperatives. Alternatively, minor changes in the cooperative societies Acts and bye-laws of these cooperatives can help to undertake this model.

Experiments with Post Offices

Mr. Vivek Kaul has already given an elaborative and practical note on the possible role of Post offices in financial inclusion. We know that the experiments of micro financing through Post Offices in Tamil Nadu and Uttarakhand are successful initiatives for financial inclusion. The NABARD has also taken initiative to cover North Eastern Region utilizing Post office model.

It is always a human factor which makes any project successful either it is Grameen Bank initiative of Bangladesh or AMUL initiative in India. Hence, my suggestion would be that the incentives to BCs and the human resource involved under any BC, needs to be lucrative so that it becomes a full fledged livelihood for them. The LIC and other insurance agents who are already in business may also be taken up as BCs to provide multi faceted microfinance services.

Need for strengthening Money Lenders Act

We are aware that the money lenders have played both negative as well as positive role in the country for the poor. The benevolent money lenders who provide loans to the most disadvantaged people at the time of crisis and emergency play vital role in the whole mission of financial inclusion. These money lenders could be taken up under the purview of Business Correspondents. The banks are having the strength of formal systems and faith of poor whereas

Money lenders do have information base of poor as their strength. Under BC model both the strengths will be integrated for the benefit of the poor.

Here, it will be important to revisit the Money Lenders Acts of different states so that it can be revised in favor of poor and excluded. The Reserve Bank of India has initiated to create a framework for money lending. A draft Money Lending Act was also prepared for the use of state Government to revive their Acts. (Reference of this fact is given in State of The Sector Report 2008)

Financial Literacy and Counselling initiatives

The RBI has initiated to introduce a model scheme of Financial Literacy and Credit Counselling Centres (FLCCs) (RBI Circular- RPCD.CO.MFFI.BC.No.86/12.01.18/2008-09 dated 4 Feb. 09). The model scheme of FLCCs would be useful for strengthening the financial inclusion agenda. It needs to be linked up with BC/BF model so that the BCs/BFs could find viability of functioning as Business Correspondents/Facilitator. The mobility and reach of BC/BF up to the doorsteps of poor will be an important factor of success of this scheme. Besides promoting awareness and giving counseling for credit and savings it would be good to link FLCCs with insurance companies so that the poor can get information and counseling services from a **single door**.

Finally, a good microfinance bill is a necessity to take forward the financial inclusion agenda as it will provide more clarity related to regulations especially on the savings services.

Indu Chandra Ram, AFC Consultants International, Germany

I am in full agreement with the views of Navin in speeding up the financial inclusion through a common strategy. I would like to add the following views:

- There is an urgent need for empowering the target groups about the importance of financial ownership through continued awareness campaign
- While working out strategy, special attention need to be taken to include gender issues/women
- Overhauling of rural formal financial network to ensure easy access to these services by the target groups
- Well qualified and trained manpower is the need of the hour to enhance the process of financial inclusion
- Financial regulators (RBI, NABARD) have to play a rigorous role and have to ensure that their guidelines/norms are implemented in its earnest by the implementers

---

Santanu Sengupta, Micro Money Management Enterprise (MMME), Kolkata

I was watching the new post as well as other posts on financial inclusion from the sideline as I was pretty busy in watching and discussing the global trend in Mobile Commerce and Financial Services, which I believe would surely play a pivotal role in creating inclusive agenda in financial services domain in a great way. Nowadays, financial inclusion agenda is considered as a way out of this current situation of financial crisis. It is evident from the agenda of the forthcoming conference at Miami, Paris and Barcelona.

Financial inclusion has many dimensions. I have been telling our venerated MFI friends to take a few leaves out of the innovators around the world to see how others have switched on to Business Development Services as a pivot of further layers of job creation in semi urban & fringe areas. But lately many of the MFIs I understand are inclined to do so although earlier they used to dislike the same idea. It will be the way forward as more and more of the excluded categories will get the taste of inclusive services and they will demand more, like our ever increasing band of mobile customers.

As to the specific queries by Sameer here is my rejoinder to them.

As to the BC/BF model it has yet to take any serious root and functionality. In the case of Gcash and Mpesa the current guidelines and banks inability to come to terms of cost sharing and apportioning them for branchless banking is a area of concern. Despite the efforts of CGAP situation has not improved much. If I have to write about the BC and BF it will be a history of succeeding failures despite RBI and NABARD's genuine efforts in making it happen. And the MFI community has a deep distrust and is scared of losing their clients that are nurtured to a bankable level. Moreover, MFIs do not see enough money in it, so they have kept themselves out of business. However, there may be some success stories also.

MFIs need to come up with innovations which the big ones like SKS, Bandhan etc are moving in, gradually. But demand supply mismatch is yawning and increasing as banks will prefer the blue chip clients rather than risking their money. Also in the current situation of economic meltdown banks are lending carefully and are interested in where the money is going and at what cost?

As to the funds let us wait for the next budget and see where it leads to.

I have always maintained that a more serious all pervasive dialogue is required with benchmark weekly reports of jobs creation, vis a vis their implementation under various schemes. But all ICT based service delivery, with or without Government support will be possible once we can settle on couple of important policy steps at macro level.

For example - the 3G & Wimax auctions will rake in roughly between 25000 to 40000 crores. But even more so it will speed up e-governance, CSC & E & M commerce in a great way as we shall be freed from the land line fiasco, will in turn spurt wireless broadband as per international trend.

However, there is no data available on the likely impact on economy or job creation once the migration and service matrix is stabilized. More importantly we should utilize the funds for long term asset creation for compounded net return to the nation & the economy as whole rather than spending on meeting the fiscal deficit or debt servicing.

In agriculture, apart from many initiatives, long awaited, SHG bank linkage for procurement to marketing plan would also go a long way in flowing needy credit to them for circulation in the community for multi level utilization and benefit.

There are still many larger issues which I have not shared here. I request you to send your suggestions on the ideas shared.

D B S Prasad, Andhra Pradesh State Cooperative Bank, Hyderabad

I would like to mention that the Integrated Cooperative Development Projects (ICDPs) of National Cooperative Development Corporation (NCDC), New Delhi are functioning as effective channels for economic development including financial inclusion. These projects are implemented in different districts of the country with the objective of economic development of people through cooperatives. The ICD projects are being implemented through the District Central Cooperative Banks and therefore DCCBs are termed as Project Implementation Agencies.

These projects are useful as it covers social, economic and financial inclusion of poor living in rural and semi urban areas. Through DCCBs, the project strives for the development of cooperative institutions in the respective districts wherein provision for funding PACS and other MFIs are being made. For the project management a separate spearhead team called project implementation team is expected to assist the cooperatives and MFIs for proper utilization of the funds.

The ICDP of West Godavari district, Andhra Pradesh has made good progress in forming new self help groups and assisting the groups as per the project proposal, so that these groups can provide microfinance services to their members. The Chief Project Officer, Mr. Vijay Kumar has proposed to provide support for insurance services to these groups. I recommend that through more proactive role of Registrar Cooperative Societies and CPOs of different districts, the financial inclusion agenda can be fast tracked. A common strategy can be adopted for speeding up financial inclusion through Integrated Cooperative Development Projects in Andhra Pradesh. Since the ICD projects are being implemented in number of districts in India, it would be good to undertake financial inclusion through these projects, at a national level.

Subhash Wadhwa, Independent Consultant, Mumbai

Many good suggestions have come for speeding up financial inclusion. I am not suggesting any further measure or strategy in this regard I just want to give a note of caution. Whatever strategy is adopted, one has to be careful that it does not lead to target pushing and losing sight of basic requirements and main objectives of financial inclusion. My long experience of SHGs bank linkage programme, SGSY programme and MFIs lending, clearly points to one fact that as and when either under Government target oriented approach or enthusiastic programme, manager have gone for target pushing, the quality has suffered leading to poor impact and non achievement of the objectives. Financial inclusion through different approaches is a process involving both social and economic preparedness. Rather than merely reaching the numbers it is important to focus on the proper capacity building, not only at the delivery side but also of the receiving end. It is important to have better productivity of the capital and creating desired impact.

Sameer Kochhar

I must say that this query has generated some of the highest quality responses and I must thank you all as well as the Solution Exchange for this ongoing discussion. Quite a bit of the inputs provided have validated some of the field level, research meeting level and one-on-one interview level findings. We are proposing to present our draft report during the 20th Skoch Summit, at Mumbai on 16 - 17 July 2009 (for agenda please visit: http://corporate.skoch.in/index.php?option=com_content&view=article&id=168&Itemid=255).

Members who have responded to this query are invited to attend without any registration fee requirement for this non-residential summit (subject to seat availability). Requests can be made to info@skoch.in and the registration form is available at: http://corporate.skoch.in/index.php?option=com_content&view=article&id=100&Itemid=161

Many thanks to all who contributed to this query!

If you have further information to share on this topic, please send it to Solution Exchange for the Microfinance Community in India at se-mf@solutionexchange-un.net.in with the subject heading "Re: [se-mf] Query: Speeding Financial Inclusion through a Common Strategy – Experiences; Advice. Additional Reply."

Disclaimer: *In posting messages or incorporating these messages into synthesized responses, the UN accepts no responsibility for their veracity or authenticity. Members intending to use or transmit the information contained in these messages should be aware that they are relying on their own judgment.*

Solution Exchange is a UN initiative for development practitioners in India. For more information please visit www.solutionexchange-un.net.in